RETENTION POINT

The Single Biggest Secret to Membership and Subscription Growth

RETENTION POINT

The Single Biggest Secret to
Membership and Subscription Growth

For Associations, SAAS, Publishers, Digital Access,
Subscription Boxes and all Membership and
Subscription-Based Businesses

ROBERT SKROB

Retention Point
The Single Biggest Secret to Membership and Subscription Growth

Published by Membership Services, Inc.

Retention Point™, Member Leader™ and Member On Ramp™ are trademarks of Membership Services, Inc.

ISBN-13: 978-0-692-09455-6

LCCN: 2018903622

Table of Contents

CHAPTER 1

Membership Growth Comes From Retention, Not From Recruiting New Members

It's 2:37 a.m., and I'm at an altitude of 38,000 feet, somewhere over the Arabian Sea. I boarded this flight in Mumbai about 30 minutes ago. It'll be 27 hours before I'm home in Florida, if all goes well.

I'm returning from a client engagement with a publisher in India. Focused on helping the team get and keep more new members. I'll tell you about it in just a bit.

What I will reveal to you within the pages you are holding has completely transformed my life. And if you invest an hour of your time to read this book, I expect it will transform your life by teaching you how to build a program that stops your members from quitting, grows to exceed your wildest dreams and generates reliable, sustainable recurring subscription revenue. Let's end the frustration of losing members as fast as you gain them. It's time to break through those member number plateaus and scale-up your membership revenue.

Twenty years ago, my wife and I lived in a little yellow house across the street from a drug dealer. Two drug dealers actually. One had a dog, until the cops shot the animal because it attacked them when they came to arrest its owner. But that's a story for another day.

My wife and I lived in that little yellow house with our 18-month-old daughter. Sadly, it was a step up from where we had lived before.

We didn't have a lot of options. We owed more money in credit card debt than we earned in a year of work. Our minimum monthly payments across the different cards were more than we made in a month. And when my wife had our daughter, she had to quit her job because after the cost of daycare, she'd earn less than $4.00 an hour working full time as head cashier at The Home Depot.

Today we live in a beautiful home. We have a gorgeous back yard with a pool and a fountain where I can listen to water flowing over rocks as I relax in a chaise lounge reading a book and smoking a Partagas #10 cigar. A treat I don't enjoy frequently enough.

My clients travel to see me from across America and around the world. And in some rare cases, I've been bribed to travel to their offices. Today I'm returning from Mumbai. It's a long trip, but not so bad in business class. It's a lot like sitting in my reading chair at home—if my home was a metal tube seven miles up in the sky.

Nonetheless, I'll have a rare 27-hour period when I won't be disturbed. My meals will be brought to me. There's a lavatory just 10 steps away. Drinks are available for the asking.

Within an hour of reading, I'm going to reveal to you the membership retention strategies that got my daughter, my wife and me out of that little yellow house and into the home we enjoy today.

My goal over the next 27 hours is to create a draft book manuscript that lays it all out for you and makes it easy for you to follow. Most of all, I'll keep it brief! My ego wants me to write another 75,000-word book, ask my agent to sign me up with another publishing deal with a five-figure advance and market my way to another best seller.

Instead, I'm going to write a book YOU want. For you, I'm investing the next 27 hours into creating a tool you can consume within an hour that will enable you to experience a transformation similar to the one I help create for my clients. And when I get back to the comfort of my home, I'll edit, cut and remove all the blabbering excess to distill this book down to the ideas you can implement right now. Grab yourself a cold drink and within an hour of reading, you'll know exactly what it takes to stop your members from quitting and to grow your membership by becoming a Member Leader.

CHAPTER 2

The Slight Change That Stops Your Members From Quitting and Grows Your Recurring Subscription Membership Revenue

I had a decision to make. Although I had gone to school to become a CPA, I took a job as a bookkeeper at a consulting company to membership associations. Just five years later, in 1999, married, with our daughter, Samantha, 4 years old and our son, Robert William, a newborn, I had to make a big decision. It would determine the course of my life.

Do I go back to a career as a CPA, or do I double down on this membership stuff? My role in the company had grown considerably over the last few years. And now, I was forced to make a decision. Buy the company or move on to another opportunity, possibly back to pursuing the CPA career I'd previously left behind.

Membership is a great business model in concept. You get a customer and your customer renews each year. While working for that association consulting firm, I discovered direct response copywriting. I wrote my first membership sales letter in 1996, sitting at my coffee table with a copy of Dan Kennedy's book *How to Write a Sales Letter* next to me on the couch. I would read a chapter and then do what it said, writing a section of the sales letter on my laptop, which back then was the size of a briefcase and 10 times heavier.

It worked; I got new members. And I began writing sales letters for more than 37 different membership organizations over the next few years. I bought the company, and it began to grow, for a time.

The internet revolution was getting started, challenging the status quo. Web-based companies began delivering what membership associations had been delivering for the previous five decades. And they were doing it better. Although I'd become great at getting new members, they were quitting just as fast.

Everything turned around for me when I stopped chasing new members to focus on creating member relationships instead.

I moved the finish line. For me the goal stopped being a new member sign-up. The new goal was getting a 12-month member.

In years past I would focus a lot of time and energy on getting a new member. Then when someone said "yes," I'd celebrate. Then move on to getting the next new member.

Can you imagine if you did this in dating? You'd be going on a first date every night. Happy you got there, but then instantly moving on to the next first date.

Instead I focused on the first year of membership. At that time I was selling annual memberships. Thus, members had to pay annual dues to become a member. I moved my finish line out a year, to when that new member renewed his dues, called "conversion." *How many first-year members convert?* became the key question.

This meant my work wasn't complete until a member renewed one year later. And what we found is that if a member retains membership and engagement for a year, there's a 90% chance he'll be your member for life.

In the years since, I've expanded beyond membership associations into for-profit membership programs, launching my own membership in 2006 and selling it in 2012. I've helped to grow more than 1,000 membership programs in the last two decades. I've worked with programs that use various offers: free trials to get new members; monthly continuity from $9.97 to more than $4,500.00; and annual membership dues from $20.00 to $20,000.00.

The key to retention for all of these programs is what happens AFTER your new member joins. Handling your new member correctly can increase your new member lifetime value by three to ten times. This completely changes the economics and stability in your business.

With a higher lifetime value, you can invest more to get new members. This increased marketing spend gives you far greater reach than your competitors. You are able to grow faster and reach people you'd never be able to reach otherwise. Plus, with more members, you get more referrals, the other services you offer get higher purchases and you have the opportunity to attract sponsors and other outside money to fuel your business.

This change allows me to triple, quadruple and even quintuple a membership program within a year. Few believe it before it happens. After years of running your own membership, you may find it impossible to imagine someone like me, someone who knows nothing about your membership, being able to walk in and triple your membership over the next 12 months.

Approach this book with an open mind. I am writing this to share everything you need to transform your life the way these secrets have transformed mine. And I've distilled it to a one-hour read.

My kids are in college now. My daughter is pursuing her doctoral degree in science education at Florida State University. My son is studying business in the honors program at the University of Florida. My wife and I are now happy empty nesters, living in our beautiful home with a resort-like pool just steps from the living room, in a safe neighborhood. We have long since paid off our vehicles and credit cards. All because of what I will reveal to you in this book.

That is the real power of this information. To transform your life from frustration and fear of high churn rates into peace of mind and security because you have a vibrant tribe of members who would miss you and come looking for you if your communications disappeared for even one month.

Most Membership Marketers churn through new members, hoping some stick, because they don't understand the difference between customers and members. Member Leaders get members to the Retention Point by building relationships with members, one by one, at scale, through their automated Member On Ramp system.

A small change of perspective will open you up to a huge amount of growth. If you'll give me an hour to learn how to transform your membership program from a series of "one night stands" into a tribe of lifetime relationships, I'll give you the next 26 and a half hours to distill what I've learned over the last two-plus decades.

CHAPTER 3

Finally Revealed, How to Turn Membership Quitters Into Lifers Who Grow Your Revenue by Becoming Members of Your Vibrant Tribe

You know those members of yours who love what you deliver? They can't get enough, they tell everyone they know about you and they buy everything you offer. These are the "Lifers." Then there are the "Quitters." The Quitters stop opening your email, don't use what you provide and then they quit (sometimes asking for a refund). This program reveals how to create more Lifers and repel the Quitters before they cost you time and money on wasted fulfillment.

The Retention Point is the moment when your members become so emotionally invested in what you deliver, they become Lifers. By reading the rest of this book over the next 57 minutes, you'll understand the exact steps to identify your Retention Point. Why it happens and how to make it happen more often, on purpose.

You'll discover the thinking that prevents Membership Marketers from ever achieving maximum growth within their programs. And what Member Leaders do differently to create programs that far outstrip all expectations.

You'll also discover:

- The five fallacies of membership retention that most subscription businesses implement that actually INCREASE member churn rates.

- Five case studies of subscription business turnarounds (or successful launches) including a publisher, a subscription box, SAAS, an association and a charity/nonprofit.

- Simple tactics you can swipe and deploy within your membership program to improve retention.

- How to achieve 90% to 98% annual renewal percentages, even if you believe this is completely impossible for your business.

- The single biggest myth subscription companies believe that kills membership growth.

CHAPTER 4

Getting Your New Members to the Retention Point Is the Secret for Fastest Membership Growth

Most Membership Marketers think they may have one or two competitors in their niche that are selling a similar product to a select group of customers. Fact is, your competition is a lot bigger, a lot better financed and way ahead of you.

You are competing with the best attention seekers in the world. Right now there are hundreds of engineers in Silicon Valley trying to engineer apps and games to make them so addictive that users never quit. You also have news producers at Fox News and MSNBC along with countless bloggers trying to capture and keep consumers' attention to generate ad revenue. And depending on who you believe, you have thousands of Russians trying to distract attention away from what's real as well.

Added to all this, you've got entertainment executives trying to write stories that captivate viewers. And if you own an upstart platform that's trying to get viewers to "cut the cord" and give up their cable television to become dependent on your programming, you'll spend some time and energy figuring out what's addictive.

You'll be fascinated by Netflix data published by *Wired* magazine that shows when a series becomes addictive.

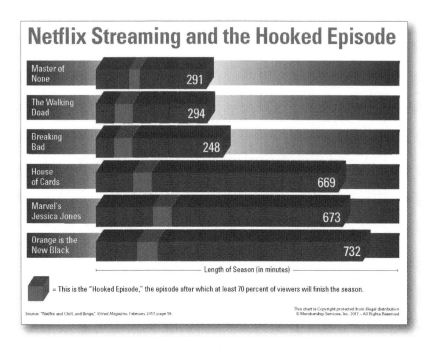

The chart shows the length of each series in minutes together with cubes representing each episode. The light gray cubes represent the "hooked episode." This hooked episode is the episode after which 70% of the viewers complete the entire series. While some viewers complete the series within a week, others savor the show over several months. Yet after the "hooked episode," 70% stick with the series until the end.

This brings up an important question for you: At what point do your new subscriber members become hooked?

You see, this is the exact same pattern you have with your Lifers; they've become so emotionally invested that they've reached the Retention Point. This is the point where 70% to 80% become subscribers for life.

However, you have many times that number of subscribers who start but then disengage within the first few weeks or days.

Membership Marketers leave the Retention Point to chance. Few even track the numbers necessary to determine where their Retention Point is.

Armed with the Netflix data, producers and writers are writing the first episodes of their programs to move that "hooked episode" earlier in the series. There's detailed analysis about what elements get viewers hooked, such as having one well-developed main character versus several characters in the program. Does there need to be a fast-driving plot where a lot happens, or should there be a mystery where facts are slowly revealed to the audience?

The quicker a viewer gets hooked, the more people who start the series will stay to the end. They are so engaged that they talk about the show with their friends, post about it on social media and tweet to the producers and actors. This leads to the producer receiving plenty of money to film the next season.

Same with your Retention Point. Getting your subscribers to the Retention Point faster is the secret to slashing churn rates.

Moving your Retention Point earlier in your subscriber life cycle is the key to long-term growth. The Retention Point is when your subscriber decides that he wants to be a member of your tribe, that he's engaged and he's going to do what it takes to succeed. Your subscriber rarely has a visible success that you or I could recognize. Instead, he makes a decision.

I've dedicated my career to helping my clients accelerate the Retention Point. And you are holding the result of more than two decades of work in nonprofit, for-profit, publishing, products, monthly continuity billing and annual memberships, all focused on engineering the combination of value, communication and community necessary to get your members to that Retention Point.

You move subscribers to the Retention Point by
1. inspiring them to improve themselves,
2. giving clarity over their pathway to improvement,
3. helping them take the first step and
4. revealing your unique personality.

When you are intentional about these components of your new subscriber welcome, you can move your Retention Point to immediately after the sale.

This is also an important answer to your question "How long should each piece of content be?" There's a lot of speculation that you should keep your videos shorter to increase consumption.

Yet the Netflix data illustrates that the hooked episode has no correlation with the length of the episode or the season. Once they are hooked, 70% to 80% of viewers will stay to the end.

"What is the optimal length?" is the wrong question. Rather, "What is the hooked point and how do we move that earlier so more viewers stay to the end?" is the right question to answer.

Let me summarize a few key points to make sure they are entirely clear:

1. The Retention Point is when your subscribers become Lifers, so emotionally invested in what you deliver that 70% to 80% become subscribers for life.

2. Most Membership Marketers leave the Retention Point to chance.

3. Getting your subscribers to the Retention Point faster is the secret to slashing churn rates.

4. It's surprisingly easy to get a lot more of your new members to the Retention Point when you try.

When you move beyond focusing on getting new members to instead measuring and focusing on getting new members to the Retention Point, your membership subscription numbers can triple, grow by a factor of five or even more.

Membership Marketers fail because they believe the wrong things about growing membership. Member Leaders succeed because they focus on building relationships with members, getting them to the Retention Point of engagement and making members eagerly *want* to belong for life.

CHAPTER 5

Five Mistakes Membership Marketers Make That Prevent Them From Achieving Membership Growth

It sounds simple enough. Create a subscription program. Instead of making one sale, get your customer to sign up for a series of purchases. Boost customer value from day one! And better yet, call your customers "members" and imply that they are receiving something valuable that's not available to just anyone with a pulse and a credit card.

The trouble is that customers don't feel an obligation to retain their "membership." In fact, the opposite is true, and they drop out as soon as they find a cheaper version of what you deliver. The bonus you dangled in front of them to get them to join worked in that it got them to join, but everything else you did ran them off as fast as they signed up.

Members dropping out of monthly subscription programs, continuity programs or memberships has reached epidemic proportions. In fact, the average retention rate has gotten so bad that many consider it a success if you keep just 50% of your new customers for three or four months. While 50% may be better than the average, it's far from an acceptable way to try to build a business.

The number of press releases touting the benefits of the membership model for businesses seems to grow each day, and yet more and more people who have tried this model are abandoning it. It's just too hard.

At least it's too hard following the Membership Marketing model.

There's a missing piece, not included in any of the books, that makes these programs work. It's the difference between a Member Marketer and a Member Leader. It's something that nonprofit trade and professional associations have been doing for decades. And it's the reason they keep their members for several decades while so many marketers are lucky to keep their members for a few weeks.

If you've been frustrated by slow membership growth, it's not your fault. All of the training out there is on how to become a Membership Marketer. Today you are reading how to become a Member Leader.

But first allow me to break down a few Membership Marketing mistakes that could be preventing you from achieving the growth you need.

MEMBERSHIP MARKETING MISTAKE #1:

Give Members More Value

You've likely heard that you keep your members by giving them more value. And if you are seeing members quit, one of the first things most people will tell you is to deliver more value to your members.

Heck, this is an epidemic even within the nonprofit association world, and you'd think of all people, they would know better.

Here's a simple example. If you deliver a 12-page newsletter each month, double it to 24 pages and you'll cut your churn rate in half, right? No, more value doesn't equal more retention. This is the same whether you are delivering subscription boxes, SAAS, digital access or anything else.

Value is like water. Too much water is just as bad as too little. Floods, mud slides and tsunamis are three quick examples of the destruction that too much water creates. It's the same with value.

Retention Point™ Accelerator

VALUE
is like water;
too much is just as bad as too little.

When you deliver too much value, your member becomes overwhelmed. Your member starts feeling bad that he isn't using what he purchased, and so he wants to quit. Does it matter that other members are easily able to consume what this new member received? While that's nice for your other members, it does nothing to retain the guy who feels overwhelmed.

MEMBERSHIP MARKETING MISTAKE #2:

Send Members a Gift of Food to Make Them Feel Obligated to Stay

---

Believe me, I wish it were this simple. I've never seen anyone improve their retention by sending a box of cookies, brownies or even Shari's Berries. (Although I've been successfully bribed by boxes of Partagas #10 cigars.)

Here's a quick story that'll help you see this from your member's perspective.

It's 3:00 p.m. and you are STARVING. You skipped breakfast and got so busy midday that you haven't been able to eat lunch yet. You feel sick, have been lightheaded for more than two hours and are ready to eat anything that stands still.

You walk into a restaurant and the place is empty. After all, it's 3:00 in the afternoon. Finally you get the attention of a hostess who seats you, and then you wait and wait for a server.

Your server walks up and says, "Wow, you look hungry. Here are the entrées that come out of the kitchen the fastest this time of day, #1, #2 and #3. Would you like to order one of those or look at the rest of the menu while I get you a drink?"

How does this make you feel? Awesome, right? Someone has recognized you are in pain and has offered you the single fastest way to relieve that pain. This server would get a big tip.

What if you are in this exact situation again, but instead the server walks up to your table with a piece of lemon meringue pie and says, "Howdy, darlin', here's a piece of pie we had left over from lunch. I hope you enjoy it. What can I get you to drink?" Argh, you haven't eaten anything yet today. Pie is just going to make you feel sicker and hungrier. Pie isn't what you want. She could bring you three pieces of pie and it wouldn't help.

Retention Point™ Accelerator

Solve problems to deliver member TRANSFORMATIONS.

Your member didn't join to get a box of cookies. He joined to solve a burning problem in his life. The faster you help your member solve that problem, the quicker you'll create a long-lasting relationship.

What if instead, after your server brings your meal, you eat and feel satisfied? Then your server comes by your table and says, "Wow, you ate that fast. Darlin', we had a couple of pieces of pie left over from lunch; would you like a slice of apple or a slice of pecan pie on me as a thank you for dropping in today? Now how do you feel about the gift?

There is one place where an unexpected gift can give you a boost in member retention. Once you have made a promise to solve a problem, then delivered on that promise, a gift of food IS a plus that builds good will. Until then, it's just empty calories that do nothing for your member or you.

MEMBERSHIP MARKETING MISTAKE #3:

Use "Pain of Disconnect" Benefits to Stop Them From Quitting

Imagine your electricity is shut off—not only for a few hours, but you have made the choice to shut it off forever. It won't be long before the food in your refrigerator starts to spoil, cold showers become unbearable and life without heat and air conditioning is really uncomfortable. If you are married, a few hours, days or weeks without electricity will put a strain on that relationship, especially if you are the one who has made the choice to shut off the power and you plan on sticking to it.

The dream of most Membership Marketers is to provide members with a benefit that's so valuable that they incorporate it into their daily activities and can't imagine life without it. Better still, it's something that when it's removed from their lives, they feel a huge sense of loss or it becomes a disruption. Losing this benefit is as unthinkable as living without electricity.

These are "pain of disconnect" or "Golden Handcuffs" benefits. Most often they fail at improving retention rates. Sure, your best members get value from the program. Unfortunately, though, the majority of your new members never implement the program, they never try your "pain of disconnect" benefits and they have "one foot out the door" before they ever get started because they sense that you are trying to "trick" them into growing financially dependent upon you.

Do you know of any marriage counselor who advises that the way to create a happy marriage is to get your spouse to become financially dependent upon you? This would be terrible advice for the same reason that "utility" benefits don't work.

Members join when they are attracted to a **transformation opportunity**; they stay when they **share your beliefs and your mission** to improve the world.

Members stay when they believe they are part of something special, as though they are in on a secret that few know about.

Membership is a relationship. RELATIONSHIP trumps message. To make your membership programs grow, you have to foster a trusting relationship with your members.

MEMBERSHIP MARKETING MISTAKE #4:

Show Them Exactly What to Do, Step by Step

This is the most heartbreaking mistake. I see so many ambitious Membership Marketers, just trying to do the right thing to help their members, get caught in this trap.

If you've implemented an aggressive new member on-boarding campaign and have seen little or no lift in retention, you likely have made this mistake. In fact, 98% of the on-boarding campaigns I look at fall into this trap. The idea is to show members what to do, and then they won't be so overwhelmed with all of the choices.

Your customer service team is going to tell you, over and over, "Members don't know how to use what you sold them; we've got to show them and make it simpler."

Yes, it must be simple, but this isn't the core problem. There's a bigger issue your members aren't seeing from their perspective.

Your members won't use what you deliver until they understand why.

For some reason Membership Marketers turn into teachers as soon as a customer buys their product. Suddenly they deliver curriculums, steps to do, places to visit and, worse, books to read.

These Membership Marketers tell their new members what to read, first, second and third. They outline the 27 steps to accomplish the outcome that was promised in the promo. This is just as bad as giving your members too little guidance.

It all boils down to the difference between a teacher and a leader. How well are teachers compensated within our society? Do they make more or less than leaders? Why would you ever position yourself as a teacher? Teachers inspire apathy, studying for what's going to be on the test and doing barely enough to get a desired grade.

Member Leaders inspire members first. They focus on showing members what's possible in their life. They get members excited about their future. And Member Leaders connect members to others who are like them. More about this in a moment, but first, the final mistake.

MEMBERSHIP MARKETING MISTAKE #5:

Send New Members the Same Stuff All the Rest of Your Members Receive

I mentioned Netflix earlier. Do you love binge watching television shows? My wife and I get so excited about a particular show that we get hooked and can't go to sleep before we watch "just one more episode." But when that episode is over, we are so anxious to find out what happens next that we watch "just one more episode." This cycle repeats itself all night. Is it just us, or has this ever happened to you?

When you are looking to start a new television series, do you open Netflix, find a new show, navigate through available episodes and then begin with season #2, episode #8? No, you start with season #1, episode #1.

What happens if you start watching at season #2, episode #8?

Total confusion, right? You have no idea who the characters are. It's difficult to understand the plot details. You totally miss the subtle Easter eggs of delight that longtime viewers catch. The show may still be good, but it takes many episodes for you to understand what's going on. Few viewers will stick with a series long enough to figure it out.

But you'd never consider doing this, would you? Instead, you instinctively go to season #1, episode #1 and watch from there. You may not be hooked on the series right away, but the chances are a lot higher that you will be.

So why do you throw your members into whatever you happen to be sending this month? If you are delivering something each month, do your new members get the same thing all the rest of your members receive? How could your new members appreciate it the same as members who have been around for several months?

New members don't know what you've sent in previous months or why this particular package is unique and special, and they don't know the people behind the delivery. This creates confusion, overwhelm and, soon, disinterest.

Member Leaders know they have to start members from the beginning. Think of it like an on ramp for the highway. You get a stretch of road that allows you to accelerate by yourself, catch up with traffic and then join the highway at a safe speed. Otherwise, you'd get run over by a semi barreling past.

Confusion is your #1 enemy. Overwhelm is #2. Both are deadly and, sadly, prevalent in membership programs today.

Retention Point™ Accelerator

Member On Ramp™
gets new members
up to speed.

CHAPTER 6

How Member Leaders Design a Member On Ramp to Accelerate the Retention Point

Let me ask you a question. In your own way, within your own membership, are you making any of the five Membership Marketing Mistakes?

It's OK if you are. I see it every day. It's not your fault. You have been taught the Membership Marketing mentality.

You are about to discover what I have learned in 20 years of building membership programs. While you do a great job, you and I both know you could do a better job of serving your members. And you could do it with a lot less time and effort if you knew a few Member Leader secrets to get your members to the Retention Point.

That is the reason I'm writing this book. It's because I eagerly want you to do a better job for your members; I want you to help them grow so your membership numbers and recurring revenue will grow. This is what will provide you with the freedom and security of monthly recurring revenue. Imagine the peace of mind knowing you'll start the month with money in the bank before you ever generate a new customer, plus the growth that comes from adding this month's new members to the number of members you generated last month.

You are engaged in an epic battle for attention. The device in your customer's pocket, purse or hand represents millions of dollars of design and engineering, all intended to capture attention. Each app icon on your customer's phone is backed by a team of professionals dedicated to capturing her attention and holding it for as long as possible. Our media today survives on clicks; each click gives them a fraction of a cent in ad revenue. This fuels headlines that demand attention to generate as many clicks as possible.

Enter you and your membership. You aren't competing with the others within your niche. You are competing against 24-hour news, click bait headlines and every developer in the app store. Are you doing what it takes to muscle out these distractions so your members give you their attention?

Those Membership Marketing experts may have told you that all you need to do is offer your customers the opportunity to buy your products by setting up a membership program that gets them to pay you every month. They say this creates a steady stream of income, builds stability and offers long-term wealth.

What does it really create? Frustration. Because you lose members as fast as they join, and some months, you lose more!

But it's not your fault. You haven't been told what it takes to become a Member Leader. The truth is that many of the membership programs that are held up as examples are misrepresented. The glowing descriptions talk about the value these programs deliver without giving the full picture of why members join and retain their memberships.

CHAPTER 7

How to Become a Member Leader to Improve Your Retention by 85% (or More!)

Can you imagine trying to describe in words what a hammer is and how to use it? How you hold it, how you position the nail and how you swing the hammer would all be difficult to write out without an example to go by. Examples and diagrams go a long way in helping you visualize what you should be doing. Otherwise you risk hitting a finger or, more likely, giving up in frustration.

Over the next few pages I'm going to show you Member Leadership in action. You'll see five unique types of membership businesses at work. Even though the examples span a wide variety of business types, each example is as relevant to your membership as another. Membership doesn't care what you are delivering, whether you are a publisher, SAAS, charity, association or product of the month. Member Leadership is the same in each of these cases.

Pay special attention to the Retention Point Accelerators you'll discover throughout this book. You've already seen several of them and may have wondered what they are all about. Here is a complete list of the Retention Point Accelerators highlighted throughout this book:

The **10** Retention Point™

Accelerators

1. **VALUE is like water; too much is just as bad as too little.**

2. **EVERY member contact is a sales communication.**

3. **Begin by promoting the END.**

4. **Your relationship begins AFTER you make the sale.**

5. **LEAD, don't teach.**

6. **Member On Ramp™ gets new members up to speed.**

7. **Solve problems to deliver member TRANSFORMATIONS.**

8. **Your value is the FEELINGS you deliver, not the stuff.**

9. **It's ALWAYS about THEM.**

10. **RELATIONSHIP trumps message.**

Rather than go into a long-explanation of each here, I'm going to do one better. As I give you examples and illustrations, I'll highlight the corresponding Retention Point Accelerator. This way you can see several examples of how each Retention Point Accelerator helps you stop your members from quitting.

Step Outside Your Silo to Stop Your Members From Quitting

I know how you are; you'd prefer that all five of the case studies I share with you feature a membership model just like yours. Frankly, that's human nature. We like what we know. My publishing clients are so big that they rarely look outside their own company for help, much less outside the publishing world. There are hundreds of conferences for association executives to attend, so why would they try to learn from SAAS? And SAAS is growing so quickly that its industry participants might think they have nothing to learn from the subscription box industry.

A huge part of the value I deliver to my clients is when I swipe a successful, proven idea from one silo of the membership and subscription world and implement it with my clients from another silo. To them it's magic. But honestly, it's all about having a larger perspective of the industry you are in.

The goal is the same for all silos within the membership and subscription world: attract and retain members to grow recurring revenue. Each subscription and membership silo has things it does well and areas where it could benefit from cross pollination with other silos.

While you may pick up a great strategy or tactic from the example featuring your particular membership silo, if you keep an open mind about ways you can implement others' ideas, the transformative opportunities will come from the other four case studies as well.

Becoming a Member Leader will transform your member retention from a monthly frustration into a program that keeps 85% or more of your members from one year to the next. I'm not sure where you are today, but if you'd like to keep 85% of your members for more than a year, read on to discover how.

CHAPTER 8

How the Largest Direct Response Marketing Company Communicates With Its New Members

No one woke up this morning and said, "I hope today is the day I get an email."

I remember a time when I did look forward to receiving an email. It made me feel important that someone thought enough about me to send me an electronic message.

Today, you, your prospective members and I are receiving a deluge of email. We'd all prefer to receive fewer emails, not more of them. This can present a challenge when the core product you are selling is a series of email newsletters.

One of the largest newsletter publishers in the world may be a company you've never heard of—The Agora. This 8-figure company headquartered in Baltimore, Maryland, has divisions around the world publishing financial investing advice, health information and materials on a variety of other topics.

I've had the honor of working with two Agora divisions in Baltimore, Agora Financial and Money Map Press, together with three of Agora's international divisions in India, Argentina and Brazil. I'm returning from visiting the India division right now. And in 18 hours I'll be home, but first I've got to power through this writing project for you.

There's no one better in the world at creating compelling marketing and sales letters than The Agora divisions. Their marketing is so precise that you've likely never heard of them unless you are within their target market. They use enticing online advertising, long-form sales letters and videos to promote their information products priced anywhere between $100.00 and $2,500.00. And when you buy, you essentially receive a series of emails delivering the promised content over the course of a year.

One Agora division has two video sales letters, and each one has generated more than $25 million in sales. Can you imagine? A video on a web page that sells $25 million! This one video would be in the top 1% of all businesses by revenue in the United States. And this is just one division of many.

Each Agora division has a team of copywriters cranking out new video sales letter scripts, order forms and sales letters. They have the smartest marketing people in the world generating traffic. It's a sight to behold.

These $1.4 billion companies grow by seizing opportunities. I've been working with them on what I call the "Credit Card Moment of Truth."

About 30 to 45 days after your customers buy your product, their credit card statement shows up. Or if they're younger than 40, they go online to see their purchases and pay their bill.

How many times have you been surprised by your credit card balance? What's the first thing you do? You look for charges that aren't yours. Next, you look for things you can cancel or return to lower your balance. And if your spouse is involved, the two of you team up to work together to lower the balance due.

You can't take it for granted that because your member was excited enough to buy on March 1 that he's going to be just as excited on April 15 when it's time to pay the credit card bill. That is unless you've been keeping your member excited throughout the first several weeks of the relationship with you. Getting your member to input his credit card in your order form is easy compared to the task of getting him to write a check and pay off the card balance 30 to 45 days later.

Your relationship begins AFTER you make the sale. You have a new member, congratulations. Now is the time to turn this new member into a long-term relationship. Consider the work you put into getting this new member: copywriting, website construction and possibly video production. A lot of time and expense. Wouldn't you want to invest similar resources in KEEPING that member to get him to the Retention Point? You would if you are a Member Leader rather than a Membership Marketer.

I've had the opportunity to work with several Agora divisions to create Member On Ramp campaigns.

These campaigns include:

Thank You Page

What your members see after they join is the single most important page. Is your page full of administrative details? Or is it written to help make your new members even more excited about what they're going to experience as your member?

Thank You Email

Your thank you email for new members has the highest open rate of any email you send to anyone, ever. Let's make sure it's as good as it possibly can be. Ensure that your thank you email resells your newest members on what the future is going to feel like as your member.

Welcome Video

A few years ago, we sold our products using written words and we delivered products made up of written words. Today, a lot of sales are made through engaging video sales letters (VSL), and when the product is delivered, it's an email with a PDF download. Or there might be a membership site login with PDF downloads. The energy of a PDF download is much less exciting than an emotional VSL. Consider creating a video to deliver content that's as exciting and engaging as your sales materials.

Welcome Package

My favorite approach is to deliver a new member welcome package that resells your new member on the value of what your program delivers. This way, if your member's spouse has any questions, he can show her your package of materials, and it will sell the spouse the way it sold your member on joining the program.

This package can include brochures, posters, a welcome letter and perhaps even a book to deliver full impact.

What Your New Member Must Believe to Become a Long-Term Member

You may be thinking, "Yes, Robert, I already do all this, and it hasn't made a difference in my member retention numbers."

The elements above are the "what to do." The key lies in "how to do it." Most Membership Marketers make the mistake of talking about themselves and what they are delivering. Heck, I've worked with some of the best in the world, and they can't get over talking about the products they deliver.

This is an advanced concept, and it may sound strange at first. I'm introducing it here so you can start thinking about it as you read the rest of this book.

Rather than talking about what you deliver, focus on what your members must believe to become your long-term members. This is what your Member On Ramp is all about.

Your new member joins because he wants something, some shortcut, tool or connection. The faster the gratification, the more new members you'll sign up. Then suddenly and without warning, your members' needs change.

This catches Membership Marketers by surprise. They lure in all these new members with some big promise, and then they are frustrated when they deliver more and more of that stuff and their members quit anyway.

While members join for a quick win, they stay because they share your belief system. Membership is about being an insider. About sharing in a "secret" that few know about. Above all it's about status. Do you make your members feel like they are in a special society fighting against the odds to accomplish great things?

For instance, the financial newsletter buyer will eagerly follow his greed to buy a product that reveals the next big stock tip that'll make him rich. Or the options trading system he can follow even if he's never traded options before. Or the cryptocurrency product that'll enable him to take advantage of this fast-growing boom market.

However, if you expect this member to do anything with the product you purchased, buy other products you may offer and renew his subscription, it will all be about whether your member shares your belief structure about the investing world.

Here's a quick list of what your members must believe to renew their subscription membership in your investing publication:

12 Beliefs to Buy Financial Product

1. It is possible to beat the markets.

2. Earning a higher rate of return than the market is a good thing to do.

3. Other investors regularly beat markets.

4. It is possible for ME to beat the market.

5. If I try, it's highly likely that I'll succeed.

6. The other times I've lost money or earned poor returns are not my fault.

7. I have enough education/experience/time to be successful at this.

8. Market conditions are perfect for this opportunity TODAY.

9. Today is the right time for ME to start.

10. This is the right opportunity for my investment goals.

11. I'll be a hero to my family and the envy of my friends when I succeed with this.

12. This is more interesting and exciting than all the other media I have access to.

This may not make a lot of sense if you aren't in a financial product business, which is highly likely. I present it as an example to pose this question to you: What must your members believe to become your long-time members?

This is what your Member On Ramp must focus on. For instance, financial publishers must teach their customers it is possible to outperform the ups and downs of the market, and show examples. These financial publishers must go up against an entire world of information that says the opposite. They must prove it is true or the customer will quit the subscription and put his money in an index fund instead.

There is also a long list of competing ideas that prevent your members from engaging in your membership subscription. The difference between the new members that reach the Retention Point and those who drift away forever are the beliefs they hold about the world and your role within it.

Your new members eagerly want to believe your membership is the answer to their problems. But if you flip into teaching mode, they'll get lost and bored. Member Leaders understand they must lead with beliefs and their members will follow.

How you welcome your new members determines whether or not you'll succeed through the Credit Card Moment of Truth to reach the Retention Point. Your Member On Ramp must focus as much time and effort on teaching your new members what to believe as it teaches what you deliver. How does your Member On Ramp compare?

CHAPTER 9

How Charity: Water Transforms Donors Into Members

If you haven't yet discovered Charity: Water, you should check out this organization right now. By bringing people clean, healthy water, Charity: Water is preventing hundreds of other problems, enabling children to get an education and helping people build an economy. It's an organization that's changing lives in important ways.

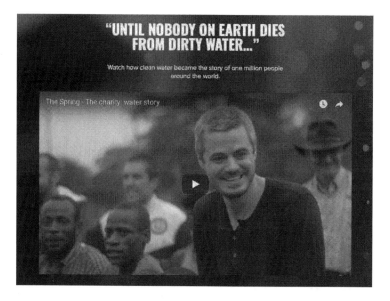

If you aren't already familiar with the Charity: Water revolution, first visit www.RobertSkrob.com/CharityWater and watch the video. This organization is doing amazing work in the world and is reforming the charity industrial complex.

Beyond that, Charity: Water has been successful in reaching a donor segment that has previously ignored charities—young people. The average age of a Charity: Water donor is decades younger than those of most organizations. These donors have made Charity: Water the single largest water charity in the United States today, even though the organization began just 10 years ago.

In the last few months, Charity: Water has launched its new membership program called The Spring. This is an opportunity to turn one-time donors into members who give monthly. Rather than feeling great about supporting efforts to provide clean water just one time, you can have that feeling each month.

The Charity: Water team engaged me to help the organization design a member experience that members would continue to enjoy for many years. There were a lot of questions about what to deliver, how often, and how to ensure the experience for members is consistent with the Charity: Water brand promise.

An essential part of Charity: Water's mission is that 100% of donors' contributions go toward water projects. If the charity begins to deliver too much to members of The Spring, they will begin to wonder why those resources aren't going toward clean water. Sure, who wouldn't love to have a Charity: Water bottle or hoodie? But if getting that hoodie comes at the expense of some young girl getting clean water, let's get the girl her water.

The Charity: Water team has innovated some of the most remarkable fund-raising campaigns in the charity world. Its donate-your-birthday campaign was new and revolutionary. It was pure magic.

When Charity: Water launched The Spring, the membership concept was new. Suddenly, rather than promoting campaigns, this charity was engaged in a long-term relationship with its members. The organization needed some standard membership systems to become member retention builders.

Essential Messages

With Charity: Water, my first task was to create a checklist of the messages that must be included in every member communication. This was a similar exercise to the one I used to create the list of 12 beliefs that financial subscribers must have.

For Charity: Water I reviewed its new member acquisition campaigns that are generating the best results. I created a list of each of the key messages within each campaign and compared the lists for similarities. In the end, I identified six key emotional drivers the Charity: Water team can use to maintain the feeling members have when they first join The Spring.

It's a list the Charity: Water team can refer to for creating its Member On Ramp, monthly emails and any content the organization creates for members. It's focused on the feelings that got members to join The Spring to begin with and what will keep them excited about the people the charity serves.

New Member On Ramp

As is common, the Charity: Water team had already put a lot of work and effort into the group's new member welcome email. Even so, there were several opportunities to improve it to increase the excitement members feel after they join.

These included outlining a new member welcome video. If many of our new members are joining because they watched a video, let's share a video with them after they join to maintain that excitement. We also designed a series of videos and communications, including one that gives the new donor a look into the process of turning donations into water projects. As I learned, creating wells in foreign countries halfway around the world is a complicated endeavor. It's good to give members an inside peek into what it takes to bring the world clean water.

Member Save Sequence

Another key system we designed is the member save sequence. Although Charity: Water permits members to downgrade their contributions, it didn't have a process to communicate with members before they canceled to encourage them to give a lesser amount instead. There's a lot of money in saving members before they quit.

Transform One-Time Donors Into Members of The Spring

One of the biggest opportunities for Charity: Water is to invite individuals who have made a one-time contribution to become a member of The Spring. Why do all the work of identifying some brand-new person who has never heard of you to become a member when, instead, you can invite individuals who have already made a purchase to join? Here's a question for you: How can your process be improved to transform your one-time customers into members who buy from you on a monthly basis?

Most Common Membership Marketing Mistake

In everything you write, say and deliver to your members, remember this above all: It's ALWAYS about THEM. Before you write a Member On Ramp sequence, invite your members to consume a piece of content or create something for your member, ask yourself, "What's in it for my member?" Ask, "How does this impact my member for the better?" And first and foremost, make your communication and content about THAT impact.

Stop talking about yourself. If you dated someone who always talked about him or herself and what he/she does, wouldn't that get old quickly? Instead, focus your communication on how what you do and deliver improves your customer's life.

Membership is a powerful relationship. You give members a sense of belonging, an identity and a community. Implementing systems that make these feelings stronger is the retention builder secret to increasing engagement, excitement and long-term recurring revenue.

CHAPTER 10

Free Trial Membership Secrets - Generate More Free Trials and Convert More Free Trials Into Long-Term Paid Memberships

---

Memberships are one of the most difficult offers to convert. Yeah, you read that right. Memberships and subscriptions are a lot harder to convert than a single product purchase.

In fact, a customer will often spend more to avoid the commitment of a subscription. Think about it for a moment: men in our society are infamous for trying to avoid commitment. Why would you choose commitment as a business model?

What if I told you I had the secret to tripling your membership? Play along with me for a second. What would it mean to your business and life to triple your membership? How much more money would that generate for you? What would you do with that money each month? How much security would it provide you, your team and your family? Do you want the secret that will triple your membership?

I'm happy to reveal the secret to you, and I'll deliver it to you in little dribs and drabs over the next 12 months.

What happened to your desire for my secret? It decreased, didn't it?

That's exactly what your prospective member feels when you pitch your subscription program. No wonder not everyone jumps at the opportunity to join!

We are living in a world of instant gratification. The 10-minute abs product was killed when 8-minute abs came out. Then 8-minute abs died a quick death of obscurity as soon as 6-minute abs came out. (And both will get killed when I release my brand new 6-second abs program.)

Some of my clients don't deliver anything to their brand new members until a new monthly product cycle comes around. By three or four weeks, many of the members forget they ever bought anything. How is it possible to value something like that?

Be 6-second abs instead of 10-minute abs for your members. How can you deliver the former and avoid getting crushed like the latter?

I learned this trick from the *Sports Illustrated* football phone commercials in 1991. This was a stupid product. I can say that because I still have mine.

Sports Illustrated ads promoted the "how cool" football phone for half the ad before ever mentioning the magazine. They sold the phone first, and then gave it away as a "bonus" when you subscribed to the magazine. They still do this today with the Philadelphia Eagles Super Bowl highlights video or other such bonus.

To jumpstart your new member acquisition systems, how can you create a "gift with subscription" that helps you drive the sale?

This is why I'm so brilliantly sneaky. It's true that I'm really good at helping memberships grow by improving retention. My true gift, however, is increasing retention and new member acquisition at the same time!

Attract More New Members to Try Your Subscription

Too many membership programs position a library of information as their primary membership benefit. This dooms them to mediocre growth rates, at best.

When is the last time you visited the public library in your city? How often do the people of your city visit the library? Do they visit as often as they do the movie theater?

I don't know about your city, but our public library is where the homeless people hang out. And all the information stored there isn't helping them much.

Your prospective members do not value libraries. Libraries feel like a lot of work. More work is not a motivating idea.

No one is wandering around the internet hoping to find eight hours of online video courses to buy and watch. You'd have to pull up the YouTube app on more than 1,000 tablets, watch all of them simultaneously 24 hours a day for 500 years to watch all the videos that are already on YouTube. Plus you'd have to add about 60 tablets with videos running to keep up with the videos that get added each day. And this is just on YouTube.

Maybe 50 years ago there was a problem with a lack of information. Today the problem is too much information. Today you don't win with bulk; you make customers most excited when you deliver transformation rather than information.

Just a quick exercise. What if I offer you the videos from a three-day seminar on membership retention, more than 20 hours of training posted online, so you and your team can watch them anytime you want? And what if I offer this to you for $5,000.00?

Oh, I'll sweeten the deal. What if I double the number of videos, and instead of giving you just 20 hours of videos, I offer you 40 hours of video for the same $5,000.00? Does that make the offer more appealing?

No, of course not. As entertaining as I'd be on video for six days, videos aren't what you want. You want monthly recurring revenue. And the faster I help you increase your monthly recurring revenue, the more value I'm going to deliver to you.

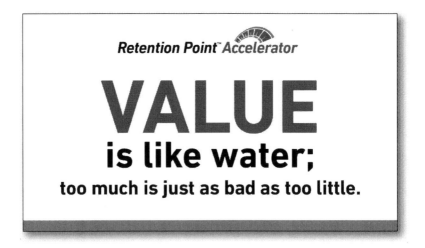

Instead, what if I boil down the most actionable, relevant strategies for high retention and deliver them to you on a single piece of paper, front and back? And as a bonus, I include examples from three fast-growing membership programs within your industry complete with sales materials, member welcome sequences and monthly deliverables so you can see the strategies in action to quickly and easily implement within your own membership program?

What if I offer this double-sided page and examples to you for the same $5,000.00? Which offer will be more appealing, 40 hours of video or the two-sided piece of paper?

Your New Member On Ramp Can Also Attract New Members

The first time was in 2002. The Florida Institute of Certified Public Accountants (FICPA) hired me as a copywriter to create a new member acquisition and renewal campaign. It was a few months after the Enron scandal, and the entire profession was in a state of depression because the controversy called into question the value CPAs delivered. Plus, the FICPA faced a generational shelf with thousands of members approaching retirement and younger members not joining at the same rate as previous generations.

First, I addressed the problem by creating a Member On Ramp that taught members how to get value from their membership investment in FICPA. To encourage new members to get engaged in the Member On Ramp, I positioned it as a guide for advancing their career. When new members consumed the Member On Ramp, they received a ton of great advice and tactics to help them build their career as a CPA, many of which were by using benefits provided by the FICPA. This meant that while the Member On Ramp was created to create new member engagement, because I positioned it as a career advancement guide I could promote it as a gift with subscription to entice new members to join. This career guide attracted the young CPAs the FICPA had struggled for so long to attract.

I created sales letters that discussed how hard it is to grow a career as a CPA, especially in light of Enron. Then I positioned the FICPA's career accelerator as the solution. But they could only get the career accelerator if they joined by the deadline date. This delivered the immediate gratification members needed to say yes. And the guide helped members get value out of the membership they just joined.

This is now my go-to strategy for member retention and acquisition. Create an on-boarding product that delivers a member transformation. Then market that new member on-boarding system as a bonus that increases sales conversions on the front end.

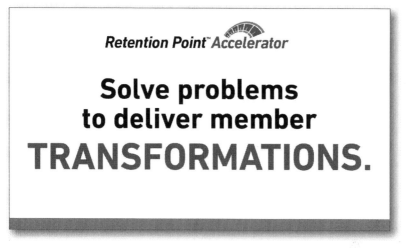

Retention Point™ Accelerator

Solve problems to deliver member
TRANSFORMATIONS.

What is the most appealing transformation you can offer your prospective members? What's the fastest way you can deliver it? Generate more new members by offering a transformation. Then deliver this transformation through your Member On Ramp to increase engagement and long-term member value.

Convert More Free Trials Into Paid Members Who Love What You Deliver

Too many subscription companies use free trial memberships. It sounds easy enough, decrease the risk for your member to give your membership a try. You hope when your new subscriber experiences your membership he'll fall in love and eagerly pay for what he's received for free.

Trouble is, the more your customer has to do something with what you deliver to experience a benefit, the less likely he'll fall in love. And thus the higher your failed free trial rate will be.

Offering free trials is an advanced marketing strategy that takes a much higher level of marketing savvy and effort to convert than asking for a fully paid membership up front. This is because what your member experiences during the free trial period must be a sophisticated combination of marketing and product fulfillment.

For purposes of our discussion here, a free trial can be completely free, meaning no money exchanges hands at the point the customer says, "Yes, I'll try it." Or it can be a heavily discounted trial where the customer pays only $1.00 or receives the product at a large discount, say half off or pay only shipping.

I've had the opportunity to work with many brilliant Membership Marketers who use the free trial strategy to scale their business. One is a subscription box company that generates an average of more than 10,000 new subscribers a month by offering large discounts for members to try its product. The trouble that sent this company to me was that it was losing more than 9,500 members monthly.

The good news is this subscription company has 50,000 subscribers. As Membership Marketers, they should be proud of what they've achieved. More than 98% of all subscription boxes fail to generate 1,000 total subscribers in their entire business while this team generates 10,000 monthly. But imagine the terror of having 50,000 subscribers and losing 9,500 a month. Would you invest in this company? These Membership

Marketers are brilliant, yet trapped by their excellent ability to generate new customers.

This company can be proud it is generating 10 times the subscribers in a month than most generate in their lifetime. Meanwhile, the CEO lives with the specter of losing almost as many subscribers as the company gets each month. When you are this awesome at Membership Marketing, it's easy to assume you can market your way out of this predicament.

This company is on a treadmill of its own construction. Marketing faster and better to generate more new members each month. But each time this company generates more new members, it sees a corresponding increase in churn rate.

Retention Point™ Accelerator

Your relationship begins

AFTER

you make the sale.

Truth is, you'll never out Membership Market your churn rate. Recurring revenue growth comes from new member retention. Not new member acquisition. A fact

Membership Marketers never understand until they become Member Leaders.

Member Leaders recognize they must use the free trial period to foster a relationship with their new free trial member to convert that trial into a paid member. They use the free trial period to connect with their new member, to build trust and to grow this member's excitement about the opportunities so the member converts.

Over the last few months I've been working with the Bradford Tax Institute to convert more free trial members to paid members. The recent Tax Reform Act is generating a flood of new free trial subscribers. There are a lot of people who want to understand the changes so they can lower their tax obligations. For Bradford Tax Institute, converting more free trials into paid subscriptions is a huge new revenue opportunity.

Retention Point™ Accelerator

EVERY member contact is a sales communication.

Would you also like an inside peek into how I've approached converting free trial members to paid? You are so greedy.

Don't Be Afraid to Use the Words "Free Trial Membership"

For more than a decade I sold memberships a year in advance. It wasn't until 2004 that I started using the free trial strategy. At the time, the "experts" taught that you don't want to talk too much about the free trial. After all, if you remind members they are in a free trial, they may just quit.

Like so much of what the "experts" say, I discovered that this, too, was total garbage. Instead I make every effort to let members know they are in a free trial. And I tell them that my goal of offering them the free trial is to sell them into becoming a paid member. Finally, I challenge them to get as much value during their free trial as they can so they'll recognize the value of their membership.

Use the Alarm Button Sparingly

Last week I left the gym after my swim. There was a car in the parking lot with its alarm going off, horn blowing and lights blinking. Nobody gave it a second look. People ignore car alarms today. When's the last time you heard a car alarm go off and it was actually getting broken into? On the other hand, how many false alarms have you heard?

You are in a relationship with your members. You are providing them what you promised to help them solve problems in their lives. There's no need to sound the alarm that some big important thing is happening so they must act immediately. Not unless it's really that important. Otherwise, they'll quickly tune you out. Your alarming messages will have as much impact as another car alarm going off in a parking lot. Your emails will become an irritation rather than a welcome message from a trusted friend.

Never Assume Your Member Knows How to Use What You Deliver

Since I was 14 years old I've been the person people call to help them work on their computers. I've got the gadgets and am a quick study when it comes to using software.

Because of a new vendor relationship, I've started using one of those popular secure password tools that allows me to store passwords and securely share them. It is totally kicking my butt. I open the dialogue box and have no idea what the symbols mean. I click around and nothing seems to work. It is constantly asking me to enter my password, and I have no idea if I'm sharing EVERYTHING with this vendor or nothing. And it won't sync passwords between the workstation at my office and my laptop at home. And I'm a techie person! How do other people figure this out?

Explain exactly what your new customer should DO with what you are delivering to them to get results. My favorite subscription box is FabFitFun, even though it delivers women's clothes I can never wear. But it also delivers something I love: an insert that clearly explains how the customer should use the products in the box.

Even if it's just a scarf, FabFitFun has illustrations with three to five ways to wear that scarf. Chances are, what you deliver is more complicated than a scarf. Are you helping your customer quickly understand how to use what you deliver?

Use the First Four Weeks of a Membership to Engage, Entertain and Build a Relationship

You are working too hard to generate new members to let them go so easily. You invest too much money in generating sales to let them refund because they didn't do anything with the product you delivered.

Use the first four weeks of your new member relationship to resell your member on the benefits of the problems you solve. Show her how terrific her life will be after she uses what you deliver. Sell the value of any free trial membership you are extending. Meet her where she is rather than trying to yell loudly to get her attention. And never assume she knows how to use what you deliver; always show her what to do, how to navigate your site and where to get additional support.

Creating systems and communications that deliver a little bit of love for your newest members is a lot easier and cheaper than replacing them every month.

If you'd like to see a great free trial conversion sequence, visit www.BradfordTaxInstitute.com and sign up for a free trial subscription. You'll learn about converting free trials into paid subscribers, and you may also discover ways to save money on your taxes.

CHAPTER 11

Three SAAS Customer Success Mistakes When On-Boarding New Members and How You Can Avoid a Similar High Churn Rate Fate

Is it easier to leap over a 6-inch step or a 10-foot wall? The 6-inch step is easier, duh.

The more you are asking your new member to do within the first few hours or days of your membership, the more difficult it will be to get that new member to the Retention Point.

Open an email and click a link. This is a low bar, and a large percentage of your new members will succeed at this task. Ask them to enter a bunch of data and create new daily habits of using a new software tool, and few of those members will be successful.

Customers will act in proportion to their excitement about the outcome they will receive. If the potential outcome is exciting, the member will take action. If the outcome is unclear and the work appears burdensome, you can expect your new member to churn.

This makes the Retention Point more difficult to reach for SAAS companies. If you aren't familiar with the term, SAAS stands for Software as a Service. Rather than paying up front for a software product, you can subscribe to the tool. For the subscriber, it lowers the up-front expense and provides ongoing support. For the provider, you generate ongoing monthly revenue as long as your customer uses your product.

SAAS companies have all the same opportunities as any membership program. Your goal is to get members to the Retention Point where they become rabid fans who love you, refer their friends and become Lifers.

The key opportunity for a SAAS company is that the more your members use your product and build habits around your SAAS subscription, the more difficult it is for them to cancel. Most SAAS companies do have a higher long-term retention rate than other subscription businesses.

The more tasks you stack up for your member to complete, the more difficult it will be for your member to achieve success. To illustrate how to achieve member success more often, play a little game with me. On a scale of 1 to 10 with one being impossible and ten being a "sure thing," how likely do you think it is that this customer will be able to leap over the wall to experience success?

However, this retention opportunity is also the biggest challenge. Incorporating your SAAS tool into everyday life takes work. The more your Retention Point depends on your member doing work and implementing, the more difficult it will be for you to get customers to the Retention Point.

Within the SAAS world there's a lot of discussion about creating Customer Success. The idea is that you must help your customer implement, use your product and experience a benefit. This can be important, but it skips over the single most important element of getting to the Retention Point.

Getting to the Retention Point is hard enough without making it even more difficult for yourself. Allow me to show you three mistakes I see my SAAS clients make.

Member On Ramp Mistake #1 - The Apology

First, the worst: A client asked me to review his Member On Ramp. I've included below a lightly edited version of the welcome screen all new users saw. I've made minor changes to protect his identity because this is as ugly as it gets.

Welcome!
We have some great updates to share!

On Monday, November 16th, SAAS sent out an email to all its members about a very important update made to the system. For your convenience, we have posted the letter in its entirety below:

Hello SAAS Members!

First, we want to start off by saying THANK YOU, as ever, for being such patient and fantastic members! We know that we have been experiencing a few growing pains lately, and your patience, your feedback, and your enthusiasm for what this system can be has been an incredible driving force for our management team. We are all eager to see the updates and changes that will be taking place in the next few months, particularly as we look forward to making our new-and-improved full-system launch at the start of the new year.

Allow this example of a SAAS Member On Ramp to be a warning to you and your team. Why would you broadcast to every new member that there have been service problems and you appreciate their patience? You should never air your dirty laundry in front of your newest member. This is worse than a restaurant posting on its marquee "HELP WANTED" or "UNDER NEW MANAGEMENT." As a potential customer, you know that place sucks if that's the smartest thing the owners can think of to write on its sign.

Your brand new member is hopeful that your product is the solution to her problems. Why would you welcome your new member with the "apology" you wrote to explain your service gaps to existing members? Your newest member doesn't know about yesterday's problems. There's no reason to create new doubts in her mind.

What if you walked up to the door of a restaurant you were trying for the first time and noticed a note taped to the door that's an apology to all the existing customers for serving them food that made them sick? Would you walk through that door, or would you leave?

Member On Ramp Mistake #2 - The New Feature

The second unforced error SAAS programs make in their Member On Ramp is to feature "New Features." Your newest customer doesn't need to know that your product didn't have these features in the past. Instead, your newest member needs to know where to start and why.

Within SAAS, as with any membership program, your goal is to get your customer to the Retention Point as soon as possible. The quicker your members get to the Retention Point, the more of them you'll keep for life.

Conventional wisdom dictates that this means the new members must implement to incorporate the SAAS tool into their lives. SAAS experts call this "Customer Success." However, there's an important step that gets overlooked that's more important for the Retention Point.

Think for a moment; what happens before anyone does anything? There has to be a decision.

Most people assume the decision to take action was made when the purchase was made. However, the purchase itself is so easy, especially with SAAS products where the initial cost is relatively small. When faced with setting aside time to implement this new tool into your life, it's too easy to back out and fall into old habits.

Your Member On Ramp must motivate your members to take action. Take the opportunity when your new member joins to resell your member on the benefits of implementing your product. Help your new member visualize what life will be like after she implements your product.

Even if SAAS companies avoid the two mistakes I've mentioned so far with their Member On Ramp, they often make a third one: starting with teaching.

Member On Ramp Mistake #3 - Start With Teaching

The single biggest Member On Ramp mistake is to focus on teaching. As if all you must do is show your members what to do, step by step, and somehow that will result in success. There are already a billion step-by-step training videos on YouTube about what you teach. Your member doesn't need you to deliver more "how to."

Instead, make the outcome that's waiting on the other side of the task as clear and as exciting as possible. The bigger the prize, the more motivated your member will be to get a task completed so she can claim that victory.

When you outline all the work necessary to create an outcome, it makes it completely obvious how much time and energy the member will need to expend to reach her goal. You've made the effort and the work easy to visualize.

The secret to getting your new member to the Retention Point is to make her life after solving her problem easier to visualize. What will her life be like when she is using your product every day? Who will compliment her as a result of learning this new skill? What will she be able accomplish with this new superpower that she cannot accomplish now?

Your Member On Ramp must focus on helping your new members visualize how great their life will be when fully utilizing your product. This is what gets new members to the Retention Point and what motivates your customers to do what it takes to experience "Customer Success."

When the benefit of the outcome appears greater than the pain of the work, your member will be at the Retention Point and will do what it takes to incorporate your product into his life and become your subscriber for life.

There are many within the SAAS world who point to Adobe as an example of a subscription model success story that does none of these things. It is true that Adobe's revenue did grow after migrating away from selling software licenses to using a subscription model. But why do users of Slack, Dropbox, Evernote, Trello and hundreds of other SAAS products try to get their friends to use those products while Adobe Creative Suite subscribers do everything they can to minimize the users and products they pay for?

Adobe had millions of users before it migrated to the subscription model. And the way Adobe implemented the change should be avoided, not duplicated as an example. Few Adobe customers appreciate their membership. And when there's a tool as useful as Adobe's tools, those customers will be gone. There's no loyalty. Adobe is relying on the Golden Handcuffs of its users' switching cost to lock them in. It won't be long and you'll start to hear about Adobe's customers leaving. And it's not a failure of the model, just the way it was implemented. Read on and I'll help you avoid this yourself.

Remember at the beginning of this chapter I invited you to estimate how likely it would be for our hero to vault over the wall to become successful. If our hero knows what's awaiting him on the other side of this wall, on a scale of 1 to 10 how likely is it that he will experience success, vault the wall and join this woman on the beach? When I do this exercise in seminars, most participants estimate customer success is a lot more likely. The man, the pole and the wall are the same. The only thing that changed is the motivation. Delivering more motivation is the secret to member success. Help your member clearly visualize a successful outcome and you increase the likelihood that your new member experiences success.

CHAPTER 12

How FabFitFun Delivers the Value That Gets Members Engaged and Retains Them for Years

---

"Exactly what should I deliver to my members to make more of them stop quitting my membership?" is a question I hear in various forms from my clients.

"To help you understand the product, we want you to know why we chose that product and how that product is going to enhance your life," said Leslie Emmons Burthey, vice president of marketing for FabFitFun, in episode 21 of the Membership and Subscription Growth podcast I host.

This answer is pivotal for every Membership Marketer to hear and understand, whether your "product" is a subscription box filled with items, an editorial in a newsletter, a digital product or a software tool your member can use in his life or business. You cannot merely deliver the product; you must also communicate how what you deliver will enhance your member's life.

Membership isn't about what you deliver. It's about the experience.

Membership is a luxury purchase. It's not something anyone needs, even if you think it's that important. Someone whose children went hungry last night is not buying your subscription program today. That makes what

2017   fab*fit*fun   THE SUMMER EDITIO

HELLO SUMMER

The Summer Box from FabFitFun includes an excellent insert to increase the perceived value of the merchandise in the box, to create a relationship connection and to transform subscribers into a vibrant tribal community.

you sell a luxury. It's better that you figure this out now so you can start marketing your membership for what it is, a luxury product.

To illustrate what that means, let's look at the greatest luxury brand in the world today, Harley-Davidson. Harley-Davidson dealers in Florida have been clients of mine since 2003. I've put on trainings for their salespeople, general managers and other departments. I've also facilitated cooperative marketing programs that get customers out on the road riding Harley motorcycles and visiting Harley dealerships.

Harley motorcycles cost quite a bit more than the competitors. And yet, within its category, Harley-Davidson sells more than 50% of all motorcycles sold. Why is that? Does a Harley get you to your destination faster? Are there Harley in-only lanes on the highway? Can you ride a Harleyin places you cannot ride other motorcycles? No. There's no "value" reason for the price premium and market share domination.

And to put the market share into perspective, imagine if Neiman Marcus sold more clothing than Target, Walmart, Amazon, JCPenney, Gap, Old Navy and everyone else combined. Harley's domination is unprecedented among luxury brands. Why?

Because owning a Harley has nothing to do with the transportation value of the motorcycle. It has everything to do with the feeling that riding a Harley gives its owner.

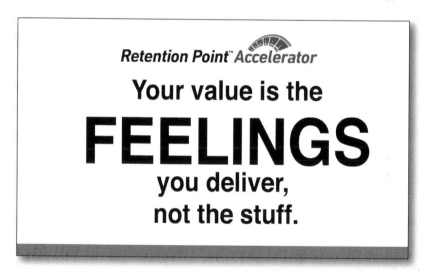

The same goes for your membership. The value of what you deliver has little to do with the dollar value of the items you deliver. In fact, delivering more value can increase churn.

The simplest example is within publishing. If you are delivering a 24-page newsletter, sending a 48-page newsletter isn't going to cut your churn rate in half. In fact, it'll be harder for your members to get through twice as much content. Issues will start to stack up and your members will quit because they already have too much to do. Value is like water—too much is just as bad as too little.

Rather than delivering more stuff, it's more important to help your members understand the value of what you are already delivering.

A Harley-Davidson owner can't imagine himself throwing his leg over a Honda. To him, it would lower his perceived status. The Microsoft Surface Pro may be a better laptop than today's MacBook, but an Apple user would feel like she's guilty of treason to touch one. If you are a college football or NFL fan, you'd eat a fat toad before you'd wear the jersey of your team's primary rival to a game.

Your membership, like any luxury brand, must confer status within a tribe upon your member.

FabFitFun delivers a subscription box featuring clothing, cosmetics and fitness accessories. And in an industry that is focused on maximizing the retail value of the items in a box compared to the subscription price, FabFitFun certainly over delivers by that metric. But where else this company over delivers makes all the difference.

Most subscription boxes rely on a postcard sized insert that explains each product within the box. Some of the more sophisticated companies include a link to an unboxing video where subscribers can learn more.

HOW TO STYLE THE RUANA

Versatility is everything we look for in summer fashion, which is why we're obsessed with the Michael Stars Ruana. Don't be intimidated by the name (it's pronounced *roo-AHN-ah*) because it's actually a simple piece that can be styled in so many ways. Plus, it's a picture perfect travel piece – just throw it in your carry-on and have multiple outfits right at your fingertips.

Check out our tips below and don't forget to show us how you're styling the ruana and tag **@FabFitFun #FabFitFun**.

DRAPE IT
Take the two front panels and drape it over your shoulders like a shawl to add some flair to your t-shirt and jeans.

SCARF
Fold the ruana in half length wise and wrap it around your neck in your favorite scarf style. You can do a simple knotted look or wear it like an infinity scarf.

SARONG
Grab the two front panels, wrap it around your waist, and tie a knot at your hip. Yep, we think it's safe to say you'll be the prettiest beach bunny this summer.

This is a brilliant example of taking nothing for granted. Some customers may become frustrated because they don't know how to incorporate a ruana into their wardrobe. Rather than leaving a customer feeling frustrated, this simple style guide transforms her into a chic beachgoer. If you can transform how she feels about herself and connect her with others who have made a similar transformation, you've got a subscriber for life.

FabFitFun exploded those norms with a 14"x11" 12-page insert with great editorial and beautiful photography. Rather than leave its value to be judged by online unboxing videos, FabFitFun has included descriptions for products, links to online videos that build relationship, a link to its smartphone app, recipes for products, a styling guide for using the products included in the box, short Q&As with the designers of the included products and, my absolute favorite, member spotlights that include brief profiles of four FabFitFun members along with a link to the FabFitFun community.

Most subscription boxes waste their single biggest opportunity in their business, fostering a relationship with their members. They get so focused on what's in the box that they don't stop to think about how they connect with the person who is receiving it.

This is a common problem. I've seen it with publishers focused on their editorial, SAAS companies that can't look

MEMBER HIGHLIGHTS

We love all our members and when you join FabFitFun you're like family. Whether you connect with us through email, social media, or the Community Forum, we really appreciate it when you take the time to engage with us. From chatting about your Add-Ons hoarding problems #addonsanonymous to sharing your favorite beauty products, you all have made FabFitFun a true community.

So here's a shoutout to some of our superstars and make sure you come and hang out with us on the Community Forum at talk.fabfitfun.com.

Susan Ortega
GUTTENBERG, NEW JERSEY
Member since Summer 2016

Favorite FFF product ever:
Secret® Outlast Xtend and Spongellé Trio.

One thing you'd love to see in the next box:
Braided leather headband.

Favorite inspirational woman:
Michelle Obama

Guilty pleasure song:
Any Bon Jovi song, I'm a Jersey girl.

Linda Baker
DARIEN CENTER, NEW YORK
Member since Summer 2016

Favorite FFF product ever:
Probably the O.R.G. peel. At 52, I still have great skin, but sometimes it feels so dull. I love what the O.R.G does to my face.

One thing you'd love to see in the next box:
I would love to see an amazing essential oil diffuser in a box.

Favorite inspirational woman:
Katharine Hepburn – love women who aren't afraid to break out of [the] mold!

Janice Elvina
ONTARIO, CANADA
Member since February 2016

Favorite FFF product ever:
Tough choice. I would have to cheat and say O.R.G. Skincare Mineral Peel Face and [the] Modcloth Loch & Key Scarf.

Favorite inspirational woman:
My grandma, but [as] for [a] famous person, it's Diana, Princess of Wales.

Guilty pleasure song:
Fight for Everyone by The Leisure Society

Jennifer Ulewski-Davis
LANCASTER, NEW YORK
Member since August 2016

Favorite FFF product ever:
Juara Body Creme and Massi Throw.

One thing you'd love to see in the next box:
A pair of luggage tags.

Favorite inspirational woman:
Sheryl Sandberg

Guilty pleasure song:
Flashdance...What a Feeling by Irene Cara

If I work with 10 clients, I may get one or two to feature their members within their publications and media. Here's a simple way FabFitFun introduces its members to other members, plus this company takes the extra step of inviting subscribers to engage within its community. For a subscription company, a community is your single biggest asset. Each box, issue or post should be focused on building your community. Subscribers quit; a vibrant tribe is forever.

past their own features to understand how a member might use their product and service companies that don't get their customers on board and using their product.

It's not enough to deliver what you promised to give your members. If you are delivering information, to maximize member engagement you must also explain to your members how to use that information to improve their lives. Whether it's a software tool or a digital download, it's all the same. What you deliver has no value until you explain how your members can use it.

This makes every member communication a sales letter for the next one. Each email has to be so good that your members are eagerly awaiting your next. And you do that by building the value of what you are delivering the same way you would if you were asking your members to buy it for the first time.

Member retention is about building the value of what you are delivering, showing your members how to use it to improve their lives and building community. Delivering more of this is the secret to improving your member retention rates.

CHAPTER 13

The Easy Steps to Get Your Members to the Retention Point

"I stopped sending out member welcome kits, and we haven't seen any negative impact."

I've heard this in one form or another for decades. Usually from an association that's stopped the practice.

Oftentimes the member kit was so bad that it was better not to send it. And rather than create an effective one, the organization stopped sending it completely.

It's the frog boiling in the pot scenario. You know the age-old question, "How do you boil a live frog?" If you put a frog in boiling water, it'll leap right out. But if you put a frog in room temperature water, he'll sit there while you turn up the heat because he cannot perceive the slow increase in temperature, and then he dies.

This is often what happens to organizations that stop sending member welcome packages. Your newest members don't know that members who joined last week received a welcome kit. They don't complain. All they recognize is that you haven't acknowledged they joined.

Sort of like when you have a great first date but the person never calls you back. You figure he or she just wasn't that into you, and you move on.

You want your member to feel like you are happy he joined your membership. Remember, your membership is a luxury item; there's no requirement or inherent need. Luxury brands are all about how they make their customer feel about what he purchased. You'll want to ensure you maximize this opportunity to make a positive emotional impact on your member.

What I'm about to reveal is the magic secret of membership, the single most important factor in keeping your subscribers and members. It's so important that I've dedicated 27 straight hours to outlining it all for you.

Every month you are spending money to generate new members. Every member who joins that doesn't get a Member On Ramp is a wasted opportunity. How many new members are you going to waste before you do something about it? How much do you spend to acquire a new member? What is the value of your member today? What if you could get five times more from each new member you generate? How long would you wait to say "yes" to that deal?

With what you are holding in your hands right now, you can say "yes," read for another 20 minutes and have this implemented within the next two hours. No more new members need to be wasted.

You put in a lot of time and work into your sales system to generate a new customer. Transforming the product you deliver into a monthly sales device that builds a relationship with your member gets more members to the Retention Point and stops members from quitting your program.

Here are the key components of your new Member On Ramp:

The good news is once you know the steps, they are easy to follow.

These are the components that get more of your members to the Retention Point as quickly as possible. Retention Point members are your greatest fans. Let's create a Member On Ramp that gets as many of your members to the Retention Point as possible.

CHAPTER 14

Your Selling Begins After Your New Member Joins Your Membership Program

"You wake up and see your gardener tending to your gardens. You play golf if you want, tennis if you prefer, or if you feel like taking it easy today, meet some friends for coffee. You don't have to rush to work; your team is taking care of every detail, including mailing your distribution checks regularly as you've long since delegated responsibility to a team you can trust, one that actually runs your business better than you did." Jay Abraham calls this *forward pacing*, a Neuro-Linguistic Programming term.

"No more long hours, late nights and working weekends; instead, by applying what you learn within this program, delegate all of the details of your business to a crackerjack team that deposits distributions into your checking account while you relax with your spouse in the paradise of your choice." I learned from Dave Dee that every proposition must promise a transformation.

During our consultation in his office, Joe Schriefer, publisher of Agora Financial, a division of Agora Global, said, "What we send our newest member is as much or more important than what we send our prospects."

Once your new member buys your subscription, your Member On Ramp has two jobs. First, stop your member from quitting and asking for a refund. And second, get your member engaged so he'll want to continue his subscription. These together are the Retention Point.

Retention Point™ Accelerator

Your relationship begins

AFTER

you make the sale.

This is your shot to keep your member; do you want to limit yourself to a few emails and perhaps an online video? Or do you want to send a package in the mail? Or perhaps combine that with a welcome phone call from your team?

While you've got to deliver whatever you promised in your sales materials, your new member welcome sequence must also be about reselling your customer on taking action. Without action, it won't be long before your member says, "I don't need what you provide." Here are the three critical beliefs your new member must have before taking action, keeping your membership and investing in your other products and services:

DREAM

Your new member thinks more about what it'll feel like to have his problems solved than he does about the investment necessary to make it happen.

Before your customer is going to take action, he's got to have a good reason for investing the time and energy. He's busy and overwhelmed already. And you want him to take time from his schedule to implement your strategies? You better paint a clear picture of what his life will look like if he takes action.

Weight loss companies have to use before and after photos to convince you to buy their programs. Then, after you buy, you realize all the food you are going to have to give up and how little you get to eat in a day. Suddenly your habits are in conflict with your desires. These companies must reinforce your weight loss dreams by showing you more photos and getting you to imagine the healthier, skinnier you. They've got to make the image of the positive impact of their programs in your life so compelling that you are willing to break old habits, plan for new routines and make different choices about what you eat when you're at your favorite restaurant with your friends.

To get your customers to make positive choices about your program, you've got to resell them on what they want. What will life look like after they implement your program? How will life be better? How will they feel when they implement what you provide?

BELIEF

Your member believes your solution works
and it'll work for him.

It's one thing to believe that something is possible. Sure, I know it's possible for some people to run a marathon within 2-1/2 hours. But there's no way I could do it. At least that's what I believe. Maybe if I trained as much as the other athletes ... Nah.

Your customer may look at all the dreams and the proof that the dream is possible and believe that it's possible to achieve, for other people. But unless he believes it's possible for him, there's no way he'll take action. And if he doesn't take action, then he doesn't need your subscription.

Convince your customer that his past failures weren't his fault. That there was something missing, and you'll provide it. Bring out any testimonials you have and/or your own personal story of overcoming this doubt to achieve breakthrough results.

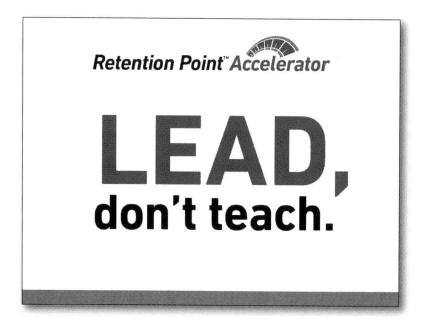

Your customer is unlikely to do anything with what you deliver until he believes it works and is likely to work for him.

GOAL

Instead of being overwhelmed by the size of the journey, your member recognizes the value in taking the first step.

When I first walked into a Weight Watchers store in 2005, I was greeted, paid my money and received a welcome kit. The lady behind the counter asked me to step on a scale, where I discovered I'd swelled to 237 pounds.

Then she explained that Weight Watchers recommends all new clients set an initial goal of losing 10% of their body weight; for me that was 23 pounds. Then she explained how we were going to achieve that goal.

My healthy body weight is closer to 175, so 23 pounds was still far away from where I needed to be. However, it was a step, a goal I could achieve and believed I could make happen.

Does your Member On Ramp do any of this? Does it paint a vivid dream, help your new member believe it's possible for him and set an incremental goal? If it doesn't, you are losing more members than you deserve. And possibly paying more in refunds than you should. These three steps will help you stop your members from quitting so you can keep more of the great new members you are getting.

CHAPTER 15

A Confused Mind Causes a Canceled Member, Clarity Gets Your Member to the Retention Point

---

Every day I receive a barrage of ideas from friends and clients who recognize the power of how I help clients. They are well meaning. They want me to share these strategies because they could help so many people. And they recognize the money I could make from products and coaching programs based on member retention.

I admit it's all very tempting. I've authored five best-selling books about packaging what you know into "information products" such as home study products, membership sites, seminars, coaching programs and masterminds. Tens of thousands of people have read my materials, and I've personally coached hundreds. Heck, I've launched more than 50 membership programs for myself and on behalf of clients. Plus I've created membership programs that I ultimately sold as businesses. Having my own membership would be really gratifying to me from an ego and status standpoint.

But all of it would be a distraction from what I love doing most. Working with clients to help them stop their members from quitting so they can reach their membership goals. With my collection of clients, I make more money than I ever could if I devoted myself to growing my own membership, as I receive a retainer plus a modest percentage of the improvement above base that my services generate.

Still, I find it challenging to stay focused on what's most important to me. The lure of my OWN vibrant tribe of people growing membership programs is exciting to think about.

Your new members struggle with the same challenge, but it's harder for them. They are brand new, so all these ideas sound equally great. They don't have a way to filter which ideas are promising versus which are too much work, and they are zipping like hummingbirds from one promising idea to the next. This confusion leads to overwhelm, which is the leading reason members quit.

There are three ways to give your members clarity to prevent them from quitting. You must address each one within your Member On Ramp to help your customer make the decisions necessary to overcome these distractions.

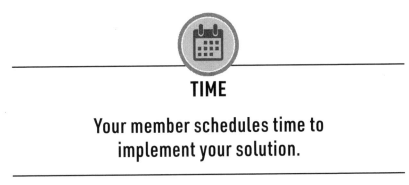

TIME

Your member schedules time to implement your solution.

The first time I started to try to sell products instead of consulting services was in 2003. Back then a thousand things got in the way, not the least of which was my clients. I was so busy fulfilling my client obligations and meeting deadlines that I had little time left to work on productizing my knowledge so I could do the work once and get paid each time I sold the product. Finally I set aside two hours every morning, from 6:00 a.m. to 8:00 a.m., to create my first product. It took me six weeks. Then as I was growing the business, I set aside every Friday; all I did on Fridays was work on my products business rather than for my consulting clients.

Often your clients have other jobs or businesses they operate to pay the bills. Or as in the case of my client who was selling to pest control guys, they are so busy spraying for bugs all day, returning voicemails in the evenings and mailing out bills at night that they don't have any time to work ON their real business.

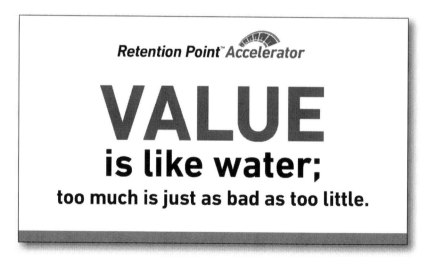

Retention Point™ Accelerator

VALUE
is like water;
too much is just as bad as too little.

You must help your members overcome this problem the same way I did, by teaching them to compartmentalize their time. They can remain busy almost the entire week.

But they need to set aside two hours each morning to build their life. Or they can be busy four days a week working for money today and invest one day working on a project for the future. Teach them how to segment their time and attention so they have clarity and space to implement your materials. Otherwise they'll never find time for what you deliver, and your members will be gone.

FOCUS

Your member eliminates all possible alternative problems and solutions; he puts all of his energy into implementing what you provide.

When you are mapping a route on Google Maps from where you are to where you want to go, Google Maps gives you the fastest route together with two other options, estimating the time for each route. In real life it's not that simple.

Your member may be trying to sort through dozens of ideas, tools and strategies promising similar outcomes. From his perspective, it would be like Google Maps providing 20 routes to choose from, with each promised to be the single fastest route.

With your member overwhelmed with strategies, it's likely you will be on the losing end of retention.

During your Member On Ramp, you've got to provide information to your member to help him make a decision about which path is the most appropriate for him to achieve the outcome he's looking for.

I could mention any of the case studies I profiled, but let's start with Agora and its financial newsletters because I gave you the list of 12 beliefs a member must have to become a Lifer. First on that list is that it's possible to beat the markets.

On this point, Agora's gurus are up against the single largest investment fund in the world, Vanguard. Vanguard's founder, Jack Bogle, teaches that it is impossible to beat the stock market. Jack's tribe of followers refer to themselves as Bogleheads. A central tenet of Bogleheads is rather than "wasting your time and money" trying to beat the market, you should invest in index funds that keep costs low and track along with the market.

My professor taught me this idea in a finance class at Florida State University. It was popularized by a book titled *A Random Walk Down Wall Street*, originally published in 1973.

Financial publishers are going against a huge movement headed the other direction. Agora gurus must address this head on, just like a copywriter must address objections within his pitch.

What are the philosophies and ideas that compete with what you deliver? Even though your new member joined, it doesn't mean he completely agrees with your philosophy. Think of your new member as someone who walks into a Sunday service at a church for the first time. That person is trying to decide if the philosophy and the people are what he's looking for. Same with your membership.

Your Member On Ramp must help your new member find himself within your philosophy. To be able to see that he can achieve his dreams through your membership.

Members never join with a blank slate. They have conflicting beliefs they hold on to. And within their first few hours and days of your program, they are trying to work through these conflicting ideas.

You do have an advantage in this battle. Your new member eagerly WANTS to believe you have the answer for achieving his dreams. Step up and show him that you do have the path he's searching for.

CURRICULUM

Help your member visualize himself implementing your solution by illustrating the steps in your journey so he can easily track his own progress toward his goals.

For decades consumers have been warned about the perils of too much household debt, yet people make thousands of small decisions and a couple of big decisions, wake up and discover they are underwater. You can tell someone to "get out of debt." But he needs a path to go from overwhelm to getting control over his finances.

I know the anxiety well. When my wife and I got married, we owed more in credit card debt than we earned in a year, before taxes. We couldn't make our monthly payments. Getting out of debt felt hopeless.

That is until Dave Ramsey created his path, the *7 Baby Steps*. Dave teaches how to transition from overwhelmed with debt to freedom from oppression by the banks and able to make generous charitable contributions. Brand new members are able to get started by saving toward a $1,000.00 emergency fund. Even if you save only $50.00 a week, at least you are on your way.

DAVE RAMSEY'S
SEVEN BABY STEPS

Getting out of debt will not happen overnight; it takes time.
Here are the Baby Steps that will get you started:

step 1: $1,000 In An Emergency Fund

step 2: Pay Off All Debt With The Debt Snowball

step 3: 3 To 6 Months Expenses In Savings

step 4: Invest 15% Of Income Into Roth IRAs And Pre-Tax Retirement Plans

step 5: College Funding

step 6: Pay Off Your Home Early

step 7: Build Wealth And Give!

There's some subtle magic that most Membership Marketers miss the first time they see Dave Ramsey's list. Most make the mistake of outlining exactly what to do for their members. Or they outline what to learn. Both of these are logical but dead wrong. This is a common mistake that many Membership Marketers make, and it increases their member churn rate.

Retention Point™ Accelerator

Solve problems to deliver member TRANSFORMATIONS.

Notice how Dave Ramsey's *7 Baby Steps* are **aspirational outcomes**. Saving a $1,000.00 emergency fund is the outcome of a lot of work. "Pay Off All Debt With the Debt Snowball" is an outcome that sounds like a great thing to achieve.

There's no mention here of creating a budget, negotiating with your spouse to determine how you are going to spend your money and then making thousands of small decisions each month to stick with your family's budget plan. No, that's hard, ugly work. No one wants to think about that, especially in the first few hours or days of a brand new membership.

When you outline the difficult work and sacrifices, you plant the seeds of doubt within your member's mind. She doubts she would be willing to make those sacrifices.

Think of it this way, what if I was trying to teach you how to diet and I told you that you'd never again eat French fries? For most people that would be impossible.

They could never imagine life without French fries. Your member is the same way about what you deliver.

For you, what you teach may feel simple. To your new member, it's as foreign and intimidating as never again eating French fries.

An effective Member On Ramp includes a curriculum for your member to transform himself from where he begins to the life he wants to achieve. The more exciting and aspirational these steps appear, the more likely your member will commit himself to achieving the desired outcome.

If your member is distracted with paying the bills, doesn't know his desired destination or hasn't chosen the best route to achieve his goal, then he's going to be frozen in inaction and won't need your subscription. For anyone delivering information, a SAAS solution or training, in addition to what you teach, you can't take it for granted that your member has these mindsets just because she bought your program. Your Member On Ramp is your opportunity to reignite the excitement your member had when she bought your program and to motivate her to take action.

CHAPTER 16

Put Your Fastest Win First to Get Your Members to the Retention Point and Transform Them Into Lifers

Memberships and subscriptions are one of the hardest products to sell. Let's say your marketing gets your prospective member excited about solving a problem in her life and makes her believe you have the solution she needs. Now that your prospective member is ready and eager to buy, you explain you are going to deliver that solution in installments over the course of several months. What, wait? I don't get the solution NOW?!? For some reason the solution is a monthly publication? Your member wants relief from her problem NOW!

I understand that you want a monthly subscriber, so that's why you sell a membership. But your member doesn't WANT a membership. She wants a solution to her problem. And if you dillydally on providing information rather than delivering solutions right away, your member will tune you out and disengage. Lost forever.

Once your customer believes in you, your solution to her problem and her own ability to be successful, and has clarity over what to do, she's ready to start.

This is one of your biggest decisions, where to start your new member.

WIN

Build confidence with simple tasks that deliver the fastest possible first win.

I've seen hundreds of products that start their customers with a long planning process. While planning is an important exercise, your member can spend a lot of time planning and not experience any benefit.

Rather than doing all that, what is your single fastest and most effective strategy for getting a positive result that works in 80% of all cases? If you are selling financial or business improvement, then give your new member the fastest way to make money.

When auto repair shop owners join Automotive Training Institute's Reengineering Program, those repair shop owners believe they want more new customers. Above all, they want more broken cars pulling in to their repair lot. Shop owners believe that if they can get more cars, they can make more money.

However, marketing for new customers is difficult, expensive and time consuming. Most of all, it's slow. What Bryan Stasch, director of coaching at ATI, discovered is if shop owners correct their pricing, they can make more money by the end of their first week in the program without increasing their current car count. In fact, a lot of shop owners are able to recover their investment in the reengineering program within the first couple of weeks simply by increasing their margins.

This is a fast win for auto repair shops; the fastest way to put more money in the bank at the end of the week is to increase their margins. This is where the first step of the ATI Reengineering Program now focuses new members.

Here's another example of a fast win. While Michael Rozbruch ships a physical product to CPAs and attorneys who purchase it, he sends out the first module via email so the new member can get started immediately. The first module is a referral letter that can generate new clients with IRS tax problems within the couple of days it takes for the physical product to arrive in the mail. Michael's new members generate new client referrals even before the package arrives? That's a quick win!

How would it make you feel if your spouse was an auto repair shop owner who joined the ATI coaching program and the shop generated an additional 10% of revenue for each vehicle by the end of the first week? Or what if your spouse was a CPA who joined Michael Rozbruch's membership and generated three new client referrals in the days before the welcome kit arrived? You'd feel really awesome about the investment, wouldn't you?

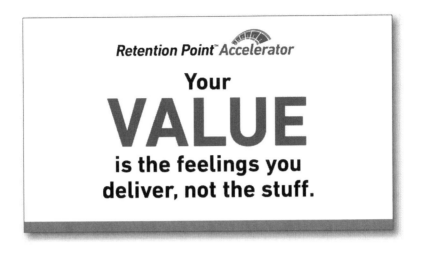

Perry Marshall is an online marketing strategist and author of several books including *80/20 Sales and Marketing*, *Ultimate Guide to Google AdWords*, and *Ultimate Guide to Facebook Advertising*. Perry has been a long-time friend and client growing his thriving membership titled The New Renaissance Club.

Perry has implemented similar strategies within his 30-Day 80/20 Reboot. Perry introduces a simple exercise that instantly eliminates more than 50% of the email messages his new members have to deal with on any given day. It's a brilliant strategy that creates mental space and relief from the constant onslaught of incoming messages. It's an easy way for Perry to deliver a quick victory for his newly joined New Renaissance Club members.

There's an important psychological component to getting your member to take action and get a quick result.

Think of it in the context of learning a new skill, such as playing tennis. You may have wanted to play tennis for years. You see people having fun on the court. But you are forced to decline invitations from your friends because you don't know how to play and you'll be embarrassed.

Your level of interest in tennis will never grow until we get you on a court with a racket in your hand, successfully hitting the ball across the net. After that we can sell you lessons, equipment and outfits.

Your member lifetime value skyrockets after your member takes action with what you deliver. Make that action deliver as large a return on investment as possible so members see and feel a positive result from their investment of time.

RECOGNITION

Engage your member into your community by delivering recognition opportunities.

This is the single-most powerful step in your Member On Ramp.

Did you ever have a teacher you truly loved? Who was always there to challenge you to become better? Even though a lot of time may have passed, you still remember that teacher's name, don't you? And if that teacher showed up right now, you'd love to share your stories of what you've accomplished since you last spoke.

This is the bond I'm about to show you. And this is the Member On Ramp element that changes everything.

The key way to change someone's life for the better is to give her a small task she can succeed with, give her the opportunity to try it and then praise her for her efforts. Whether it's an employee, a child or your newest member, this formula changes lives and grows a vibrant tribe of people who are loyal to you.

I explained in the previous section about Michael Rozbruch's program for CPAs to generate referrals. One element of his system is that Michael teaches the CPA to include Michael on the mailing list. This way Michael's office receives a copy of the referral letters his new member sends out. Then Michael's team sends out a letter that appears to be handwritten by Michael that says, "I saw your referral letter, excellent job. I'd love to hear about your results. Let me know about any referrals you receive."

This gives new members a lot of pride and a great feeling of success. Again, all before the actual welcome kit arrives in the mail. Plus it also generates a steady stream of results from brand new members. One member may get three clients with a value of $12,000.00. Another may get one client worth $2,500.00. Some get nothing. Either way, Michael is able to follow up with these members, give them more recognition during member calls and further build their confidence and connection to the membership. Oh and it doesn't hurt Michael's future sales efforts to be able to tell prospective members how quickly other members have generated new clients using his system.

I've worked with membership programs to implement this idea in dozens of different ways. While it's great to get members interacting with you, it can quickly become a fulfillment nightmare.

You could implement something as simple as a certification program where your new members complete certain levels of training. This way a member can put a certificate on his wall and get recognition from the people around him.

My clients with vibrant online communities will often invite new members to post their work within the forum. This allows new members to show their work and get feedback from other members. Think of it like your child coming home from kindergarten with an art project. You post it on your refrigerator to demonstrate to your child how proud you are of what she accomplished in school.

Harley-Davidson has this built into its culture as well as anyone, and it's one of the secrets that have been lost on others, such as Apple and Tesla. A stock Harley-Davidson comes with some chrome and accessories, but there's a lot of room to customize. You can buy home battery covers, transition covers with gold eagles and don't forget the exhaust systems or custom paint jobs. Harley-Davidson dealerships have lots of bike shows where you can bring the bike you purchased and then customized with parts you purchased from the store for others to walk by and admire. And they do; people walk by for hours pointing out to you all the cool ways you customized your motorcycle.

When you visit Rome, you'll see this same thing happening in the chapels within the hundreds of churches throughout the city. Families for hundreds of years competed with other families to decorate their chapel with paintings by Michelangelo and sculptures by Bernini so their family would be recognized as the preeminent family within the parish. If the family had a child that went on to become a pope, a painting would be commissioned so generations of parishioners would know the family who raised a future pope. (That's one proud mamma!)

The Catholic Church of the 1700s used recognition. Harley-Davidson uses it to sell more than half of all the motorcycles in the world within its niche. Every great leader today uses recognition to motivate members into action. How can you incorporate more recognition into your membership?

Above all, people crave recognition. Transform yourself from the program that issues missives from on high into a leader that delivers recognition for those who are striving to uphold your tribal values, and you'll transform your results from churn through a bunch of new members each month into a vibrant tribe of members who eagerly refer you to their friends.

UPSELL

Invite your member to accelerate implementation by investing in additional products and services.

This is always a strange topic for me to weigh in on with such a diverse audience within the membership world. Selling something to your members who just joined. For

SASS or association professionals, the concept of pitching something to a new member makes them throw up a little in their mouth. For the publishers I work with, the upsell opportunities are the entire reason they recruited a new member in the first place.

If you aren't quite ready for the concept of upsells, read on. It can be a game changer for your membership growth.

First, let me clarify what I'm talking about. You may be selling membership as a standalone purchase or as a free trial. All good. Or you may have a series of automated upsells as part of the initial transaction. For instance when people join your membership, you immediately offer them an opportunity to buy a course. I'm not talking about any of that. I completely support your efforts to maximize the dollar size of your initial member transaction. The upsells I'm referring to here come after the initial transaction as part of your fulfillment in your Member On Ramp.

I've found that when you offer an upsell to your new members during your Member On Ramp, the new members who invest in the upsell product retain at a much higher rate. This makes sense, right? They are making another investment in what you offer, so these members are more committed to succeeding.

But there's another observation that's not so obvious. The members who are offered an upsell and don't buy also have a higher retention rate. Yes, that's right, the upsell, when done well, almost always results in an improvement in retention, even from those who don't buy the upsell. From what I can gather from speaking to members who don't buy the upsell, giving them an opportunity to buy something more expensive makes the membership they have look like a better value. They think, "I can't afford that big program, and I'm getting what I need at a much lower price."

Retention Point™ Accelerator

EVERY
member contact
is a sales communication.

There are two keys to making upsells really work as part of the Member On Ramp. First, you must always deliver what you promised as part of the initial sale, and make it awesome. If your initial fulfillment sucks, your retention is crap and upsells won't help you. It's a trust thing. If within your sales letter you promised the sun, the stars and the moon, you better deliver them, in that order. This creates trust that sets up the upsell and gets you to the Retention Point.

Second, position the upsells as an accelerator for the core transformation. For instance, weight loss. Your program must deliver everything you promised in the way of a weight loss transformation to your member. But perhaps the upsell you offer helps your member achieve it faster and with less effort, or he gets more one-on-one support.

My clients who automate and split test their new member upsell path together with their Retention Point key performance indictors perform the best. Having this automated allows you to split test what works so you can maximize promise fulfillment, member engagement and lifetime value improvements.

Upsells generate better results for your members. It helps them get to the Retention Point whether they buy the upsell or not. For you, it quickly increases your lifetime member value. The higher your member value, the more you can invest in generating new members. The more marketing investment, the more new members you can reach. The more new members you reach, the faster your membership grows. And now that you've got the Retention Point dialed in with your Member On Ramp, your membership can triple or grow five times with this automated membership scaling machine in place.

The Single Biggest Member On Ramp Mistake That Prevents Most Membership Marketers From Ever Reaching the Retention Point

I recently received a welcome package to review. It was written by the direct response copywriter who has earned more money in performance royalties from what he's written than any other copywriter today. His letter starts out, "I am proud to welcome you to the …"

Grrrr. He made the same mistake my newest marketing assistant made. Why would you welcome a new member by starting with the word "I?" Instead, focus on your new member.

Retention Point™ Accelerator

EVERY
member contact
is a sales communication.

Have you ever started a relationship with someone who talks about himself all the time? How does it make you feel? Like you want to get away from that person as quickly as possible, right? It's the same when you talk about yourself and what you deliver within your Member On Ramp.

In this book I've used the word "you" 1,343 times. And the word "I" 170 times. As soon as you can, look at your new member welcome emails and letters. How many times do you use the word "you" versus "I"? Chances are you've talked about yourself a lot.

Challenge yourself to start your letters with the word "you." Transform your welcome from "I am proud to welcome you to the ..." into "Your life will never be the same now that you are a member of ..." The copywriting may not be great here; I've been writing for 18 hours now.

Nothing you do to get your members to the Retention Point will improve unless you make your member the subject of every sentence and paragraph. Stop writing about you and what you deliver. Always write about your member and how her life will improve when she uses what you deliver.

Boring But Important

I'm running out of time and tempted to leave this out; it's a list of important Member On Ramp components that are not exciting. This is a list of "common sense" items that are routinely left out of most member welcome processes.

I'm going to show you examples from printed new member welcome kits because it gives you something interesting to look at. While I love sending a thoughtfully created new member welcome kit in the mail to new members, everything in the list below could be done through a welcome video or email sequence. Don't feel like you are required to send a welcome kit.

What I usually suggest is to split test your Member On Ramp. Create the messages and deliver them through an email series. Watch your numbers for an increase in member lifetime value. Then split test videos and mailed member kits, looking to see how these elements impact lifetime value. When you find the increase in value more than covers the increased fulfillment cost of a physical kit, then you know the printed and mailed new member welcome kit is a winner.

Build the value of your people

Here's a page from the Automotive Training Institute's new member welcome kit that explains what it takes to become a coach.

What It Takes to Become a Coach for Automotive Training Institute

With a combined 325 years of experience in the auto repair business, ATI's coaches are prepared to help you make your dreams a reality through your business. Each coach has a minimum of 15 years' experience actually running an auto repair shop. And not just experience, but successful experience implementing the same strategies and techniques they are teaching you.

Plus, your coach receives extensive training from ATI, including a step-by-step process that will challenge you to completely re-engineer your shop without overwhelming you with too much work. This process was refined and improved based on hundreds of shop owners participating in the program. You are the beneficiary of years of lessons learned.

There is no team better prepared to help you. With their real-world practical experience in auto repair shops, their specialized training and their experience with other ATI clients, ATI's coaches are uniquely qualified to help you achieve your dreams through your auto repair shop.

When a new member joins your program, she has no idea how you select and train your team. In dozens of other instances when she has made a purchase, she has been passed off from a salesperson to someone else who doesn't know her and has no idea what she's trying to accomplish.

ATI explains the background and experience of ATI coaches to its new members. If you don't build the value of your people, your new member will have to rely on her past experiences in other situations to judge your people. And likely your people will be engaging with a new member who is expecting the worst.

Introduce your cast of characters

This happens a lot in associations and publishers where there are a lot of different people who send out emails; it's bewildering to new members. Have you ever met someone who passed along your email address and phone number to several of their friends, and then those friends all started to send you messages? No, you probably haven't because that would be really strange.

Why would you bring in a new member, and then have several different random people send him emails? It may not appear random to you because you know who the people are and what they do. But to your member it can be completely disorienting.

Your Member On Ramp should include a directory of the people your member will be hearing from. Think of it as if your new member has come to your home for a party. At the party you have a bunch of friends you'd like to introduce so they can relax and enjoy each other's company. You wouldn't leave your guests to fend for themselves to figure out who everyone is. Don't make this mistake with your new members. Introduce each of the people your member will be hearing from.

Include member success stories

The single most important thing you can deliver to your member at any time, but especially during your Member On Ramp, are member stories illustrating your tribe's values. On the next page you will see a page from a member welcome kit for Rich Dealers, a marketing company that's effective at getting car buyers to show up at car dealers ready to buy a nicer, newer car.

The team at Rich Dealers is brilliant; they were already using member profiles in their marketing materials. However, they hadn't yet implemented them within their Member On Ramp.

People love reading about people. *People* magazine has more than 3 million subscribers while *Business Week* has less than a million. Make your publications and especially your Member On Ramp about people overcoming challenges, using your products and services to succeed and illustrating your tribal values.

★ ★

KEVIN POWELL: RACING TO SUCCESS

KRAZY RESULTS, KRAZY FAST!

Krazy Kevin Powell is really anything but crazy. In fact the only thing really crazy about Kevin is the phenomenal success he's experienced since joining Rich Dealers® (and that he's a winning driver on the NASCAR tour). **After joining Rich Dealers® in October of 2009, Kevin increased his net profit by almost $400,000 in just over one year. Now that's KRAZY!**

Kevin is #1 on the race track and at the dealership. He drives hard and fast on the track and in life pushing himself and his team to excel beyond their normal limits.

Kevin started out on the racetrack. Growing up racing cars and go-karts, young Kevin earned money detailing cars, progressing to working on cars in the body shop. Eventually he left home for college where he returned again to the car business, this time as a salesman.

After graduating college, Kevin began work for Pat Ryan and Associates as a Financial and Insurance Specialist, teaching finance managers how to sell insurance. Kevin became 1 of the top 3 trainers in the company. Eventually Kevin found himself in Winston-Salem, NC and a friend there encouraged him to change career paths and come to work for him at his dealership, assuring Kevin that he would never achieve his dream of owning his own dealership without first running a store.

That logic made sense to Kevin and with this goal in mind, Kevin began his career again in the auto industry, working his way up through the ranks, from Used Car Manager to New Car Manager to General Sales Manager to General Manager. After working as a General Manager for a few years, Kevin decided it was time to pursue his

ultimate career objective, to own his own dealership. At the time, Kevin worked with the owner of the store and became a minority partner and a Vice President, running 4 Saturn stores. Then when the majority partner decided he wanted to sell the big store, Kevin jumped on the chance to finally own his own store. "I didn't have the capital to buy the big store so I bought the smaller store that I have now in 2005."

Kevin's hard work, drive and vision soon made his modest dealership a success. Kevin states, "Being a 1st generation car dealer and running a small dealership in the middle of nowhere, very blue collar and a 1 man show, I was doing everything myself. But we were selling cars and making money. When I first took over the store, coming from running a 350-car store to a 40 to 50-car store, it was like I was on vacation. I'd get home from work at 7 o'clock at night and my wife wanted to know if I was sick."

Then during the recession, his store experienced what many other dealerships faced—volume was cut in half, and as a result of that, Kevin let go of half his employees. "It got pretty ugly, pretty quickly. Nothing I did moved the needle at all. I was panic stricken. I don't have any rich uncle or rich daddy or anybody to catch Kevin Powell. If I make a mistake, it's all on me. If I go down, I'm going to go down in flames."

Journey To Rich Dealers®

At that point, Kevin looked hard look for a way to turn things around at the store.

This journey led him to Rich Dealers®. Kevin admits, "I was very skeptical because if I make the wrong decision, it could wipe me out. Once I did the research on the guys, I realized this was something I wanted to do because it was different and what I was doing then wasn't working. Rich Dealers® taught me the difference between push marketing and pull marketing. I've learned it's tough to make a living off the commodity shopper. **I've learned to push people into the market and now understand that certain people don't have an intention to be in the market but they are looking to solve a problem.** They don't think they can buy a car because they owe too much on their car, need cash down, have bad credit or

Here's the first page of a multipage member success story. Rich Dealers uses these success stories to illustrate its tribe's values and to engage new members during the Member On Ramp.

Raise your member's social status

You must disclose your "big idea" reason why you exist, beyond trading stuff for money. With Harley-Davidson it is about freedom and expression of individuality. Apple clearly communicated its mission when it introduced the Macintosh computer in the famous 1984 Super Bowl ad.

We've seen the big ideas that drive the memberships I've opened up for you within this report. For Agora, its mission is to be the source of unbiased financial investment information. Charity: Water is focused on eliminating diseases and enabling economic growth by providing water to everyone in the world. For FabFitFun, it's all about making it fun to be healthy.

Many clients tell me they don't have a mission. They say the only reason they started their business is to make money. While the role of a business is to generate profit for owners and shareholders, you get up and go to work for something bigger than money. Within your work there's something you feel passionate about that's more important to you than increasing your stack of cash. Let's communicate that to your new members in your Member On Ramp.

I recently created a comprehensive membership rejuvenation for the Florida Farm Bureau that turned it around from declining members to membership growth. It included a Member On Ramp, a value build for the benefits FFB delivers, a renewal campaign and something that was not part of my agreement, but I threw in because I knew how important it would be to the results, a mission.

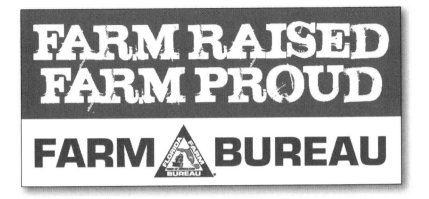

In my surveys and interviews with the Florida Farm Bureau's board, local leaders and canceled members, I found an immense pride in the products farmers produce. All this while the media and our culture denigrate farm-raised products. Add to this the portrayal of farm people as simple or backward. They are actually some of the smartest, hardest working people I've had the privilege to know.

While the Florida Farm Bureau invests heavily in advocating for farmers, it's a difficult message to communicate as there's a lot of legal jargon that leadership may be comfortable with but the average member doesn't care about. This was an opportunity to communicate the Florida Farm Bureau's advocacy efforts succinctly and to make the membership proposition about something more than providing access to benefits in exchange for money.

With "Farm Raised, Farm Proud," the Farm Bureau promotes the people and products raised on farms. This program has been embraced by members, and it makes my day when I see a truck or a car with one of these stickers.

This can also be done through certifications, member-only logos or anything that allows your members to improve their social status because they belong to your organization.

How can you make your members proud they are part of your membership? Not because of the stuff they have access to, but because being your member raises their status in life?

Consider the key stakeholders in your member's life

Your member doesn't live in a bubble. Chances are your member has a spouse. If you are selling to a businessperson, he or she likely has employees, vendors and advisors.

Even though your member may have taken the initiative to buy your subscription, there's likely others involved in implementation. Each of these people has influence on whether or not your member engages in what you deliver, and they can have a huge impact on your member's lifetime value.

Here's a page from the Automotive Training Institute that's written for the new member's spouse:

Growth Is a Team Effort

At ATI, we understand that everything you accomplish in your life is a result of the amount of support and encouragement you receive at home. And the better your spouse or significant other understands what you are doing, the more he or she is able to support you.

It's for that reason Chubby and your coach encourage you to bring your spouse or significant other with you to the ALIGN YOUR SHOP FOR PROFIT training program. While some of it will be boring shop talk, your spouse will enjoy a lot of the other parts of the training. And, if you have questions about what was said, four ears are better than two.

With children's activities and other work commitments this may be impossible. If it is, no problem. But if it is possible for you to bring your spouse or significant other, you are welcome to bring him or her as your guest.

Plan a Trip to Our Nation's Capital

Over your 30-month Re-Engineering Program, you'll have the opportunity to attend three training programs as well as your first 20-Group meeting. For one of those four trips, plan a visit to Washington, D.C.

Enjoy the cherry blossoms in March or visit the monuments, museums and memorials year-round. Washington, D.C., is a 40-minute drive away, or you can travel by train if you prefer.

The member just invested $45,000.00 to join ATI. Plus, there are several trainings to attend in the Baltimore area. The spouse's first reaction is going to be to protect, to prevent a disappointing loss.

You thought you had to worry about your competitors. And before the sale, you do. But after your new member joins, your chief competition is the stakeholders that surround your member.

Consider the people your member will need to engage to implement what you deliver. Ensure your Member On Ramp includes messaging that helps those people recognize the value of what you deliver and to find their role in helping your member succeed.

CHAPTER 17

How to Use Your Member On Ramp to Increase New Member Sales

As much as I talk about retention, I know what is really exciting to you, generating new members. You may agree retention is important, but nothing feels as exciting as getting a new member. You are in luck because you can use your Member On Ramp to attract more new members than you can without one.

Selling new memberships is hard. Although membership and subscription businesses are popular start-up concepts, selling a subscription offer to a customer is one of the most challenging sales to make. Think of it this way:

What if I convinced you that I have the answer to solve the marketing and sales problems in your business? What if I told you I can end cold prospecting forever? You'll never again have to scrape and hope for a new customer? No more up and down yo-yo of revenue? Instead, customers can be attracted to you, will contact you and will be ready to do business with you. And what's better, these customers will appreciate you and pay you premium prices for your products. Is that something you'd want and appreciate?

Perfect. I'll reveal all these secrets to you, in installments within a newsletter over the next several months. Now how attractive is the offer? No, you want those benefits and you want them right now! Of course you do. So do your prospective members.

It's a lot easier to generate new members for your long-term membership when your offer includes immediate benefits for your prospect.

Business owners are overwhelmed, busy and easily distracted. If you are able to get their attention, you've got to give them results right away. No BS Inner Circle publishes products on marketing for small businesses. No BS Inner Circle delivers on all of the promises I made three paragraphs above.

The core product that unites the No BS Inner Circle community is the monthly *No BS Marketing Letter.* This newsletter features case studies of members who are getting excellent marketing results for their businesses.

While the newsletter No BS Inner Circle produces has great information, a newsletter is difficult to sell to new members. When new customers get a newsletter, they aren't sure what's going on because of the terminology, principles and people they aren't familiar with. A new member could read the newsletter cover to cover and not know how to get started. He might start to believe that marketing is not for him, give up on it and quit the subscription. While the newsletter is a tremendous resource, it's written for members who have been members for many years. It's not designed as a step-by-step for new members.

I worked with No BS Inner Circle to create a Member On Ramp to address these challenges. No BS Inner Circle's Member On Ramp gives new members the nine marketing principles that deliver the fastest results, introduces new members to the people and ideas within No BS Inner Circle and helps new members implement the nine principles quickly to generate immediate results.

Rather than keeping this Member On Ramp hidden to deliver after a new member joins, we named it the Magnetic Marketing Business Transformation (MMBT). Now we offer this business transformation as part of the offer to join No BS Inner Circle for the first time. The MMBT has two main components:

1. Magnetic Marketing Lifestyle Liberation Kit - A Member On Ramp package that includes a three-hour audio training that briefs new members on the value of the nine strategies and explains the essential beliefs of No BS Inner Circle members.

2. Lifestyle Liberation Series - A nine-week training course that extends the Member On Ramp experience. Each week's training focuses on one of the nine fastest-working No BS Inner Circle strategies.

The MMBT is offered as a free gift when a member joins No BS Inner Circle at the Gold $59.00 level. This delivers a tremendous value to new members. It helps new members with price strategy, crafting compelling offers, attracting clients and measuring the results of marketing. And it serves No BS Inner Circle's purpose as a Member On Ramp that engages new members in their membership to increase lifetime value.

And because it's positioned as a free gift with a new membership, this Member On Ramp also improves conversion of new members by promising and delivering an immediate benefit.

While the Retention Point focuses on keeping your members, when you do it the way I've explained within this book, it also attracts and converts MORE NEW MEMBERS. Membership growth is compounded; you get more new members and you keep your members longer. This is where the three to five times growth comes from that I promised you earlier.

CHAPTER 18

What's Next: Build Your Own Member On Ramp to Get More New Members to the Retention Point

If your goal is to add 1,000 new members this month but you had 300 members cancel their memberships, then 30% of your marketing expense, your copywriting and the efforts of your sales team were expended to replace members you once had. Think about that effort and expense for a moment. All just to try to stay even. Thirty percent of your month's investment to keep from falling behind.

It's even worse if you are issuing significant refunds. Now you've got to expend more marketing dollars just to get back to the revenue number you thought you had achieved.

Churn, cancels and refunds have been accepted as a normal part of subscription businesses. Yes, there will always be churn and some of it is normal and healthy; you can't please everyone.

But if you consider the percentage of your marketing efforts that are devoted to replacing members who quit and replacing sales that have refunded, doesn't it make sense to invest some of that time and money into creating better on-boarding for new members?

How long do you want to continue losing so many members each month? How many months will you tolerate spending a huge part of each month's investment just to keep from falling behind? Do you see how much easier your life can be if you leave the Membership Marketing days behind and embrace the Member Leader lifestyle?

Quick Diagnostic: Is It Time to Embrace the Retention Point?

If I selected 100 of your members at random, and then I erased you from their lives, meaning you no longer charged them, you never again sent them an email and you no longer delivered your product or service, how many of the 100 would miss you? How many would come looking for you when your email didn't appear in their email inbox?

It's one thing to get noticed, talk louder, be bolder and get attention. It's something else to be missed. This is what happens when you get your members to the Retention Point.

"I don't know about this, Robert. I do most of this stuff already." This is what I hear from dozens of clients when I lay this out for them.

The Retention Point is like the high jump; 99% over the bar is the same failure as if you never left the ground. You can do A LOT of this and still fail. Sort of like the surgeon who leaves a single sponge inside a patient. He did everything right except for one detail. That missed detail makes his performance 100% deficient.

The Retention Point comes with doing everything right. And I've outlined it all right here so you never again have to wonder, "What benefits do my members really want?"

An Easy Way to Determine If Your Members Are Reaching the Retention Point

Many Membership Marketers talk about failed charges and how they can't reach their members to get updated credit card information. Their members don't miss them.

Sure, it's smart to have follow-up email sequences and to call multiple times. All these have been proven to increase collection and engagement. But this is a Band-Aid for a larger problem.

If someone from the road department left a voice mail for your member that said, "Hello, this is Joe from the road department. I'm calling to let you know the highway you use every day to get to work will be closed until you and I talk. You'll need to find an alternate route to work tomorrow unless I hear from you by 5:00 p.m. today." Does your member return that call? Darn right because she NEEDS that road. She uses it every day. She depends on it being there. It's an important part of her life. And she will miss it if it's taken away.

How about you? Are you important? Will you be missed?

Some of your members already answer this when your people email and call about failed charges. Does it take a herculean effort to get members to respond? If members ignore your calls, they don't miss you.

When your people leave a message, do your members call back to say, "Don't you dare end my membership. I love being a member; here's my updated card. Sorry for the inconvenience."? Then you have this right. And it shouldn't happen just once in a while; this is the way it should be each time you contact your members. You likely already have it happening a little, with the relatively few members who have reached the Retention Point.

This book, in just a few pages, distills exactly what it takes to deliver an experience that will be missed by your members. Something they want so much that they'll read your email, answer your calls and respond. Not just a few members, but ALL of them.

Wow, I'm exhausted. Been powering through with nonstop coffee and my focus on creating a guide you can use to transform your membership results.

There's fewer than 45 minutes before we land. That means I only have 20 or 25 minutes before I'll have to put away my laptop.

A Quick Recap of Member Leadership Principles

By now you know membership growth is about the members you keep rather than the new members who join. It costs you money when someone joins. Both in marketing expenses and fulfillment. Your only opportunity to make a profit and to have security in your business is to make that member into a Lifer.

The *10* Retention Point™

Accelerators

1. **VALUE is like water; too much is just as bad as too little.**

2. **EVERY member contact is a sales communication.**

3. **Begin by promoting the END.**

4. **Your relationship begins AFTER you make the sale.**

5. **LEAD, don't teach.**

6. **Member On Ramp™ gets new members up to speed.**

7. **Solve problems to deliver member TRANSFORMATIONS.**

8. **Your VALUE is the feelings you deliver, not the stuff.**

9. **It's ALWAYS about THEM.**

10. **RELATIONSHIP trumps message.**

Getting members to the Retention Point is the secret to maximum member retention. Make the Retention Point your finish line rather than hitting the gong when you get a new subscriber.

Membership Marketers start with a product, and then try to figure out who to sell it to.

Member Leaders start with the group of customers they'd like to help, and then create products that solve problems for those members.

Membership Marketers focus on generating a transaction or a sale.

Member Leaders focus on fostering long-term relationships.

CHAPTER 19

How Many Members Must You Lose Before You Fix Your Member Experience?

Your objective is to establish a relationship with your members—to a greater, deeper and more certain extent than other Membership Marketers can and that you ever have before, purposefully, so that each new member is inspired to bring his friends and contacts to you.

Your rejuvenated member relationship will create a business providing reliable, recurring revenue and a foundation of stability and wealth with prominence and prestige, a thriving tribe of members, freedom from worry or difficulty in attracting all the new members you'd like, and the liberty and security to conduct business in a manner that pleases you.

Achieving such objectives is possible. Many of the examples I've presented here are doing it. The top membership programs I consult with make it happen. But it is rare. Very rare. I'm describing a profoundly different member experience. It requires doing just about everything differently. Clues to just how differently have appeared throughout this book.

First of all, you've got to dismiss the entire idea of getting new members as your primary engine for growth and instead develop a vibrant tribe of members who eagerly do the selling for you. Leave behind all the heavily promoted marketing mumbo-jumbo, advertising campaigns and expensive lead funnel "hacking" that require huge investments, but deliver little membership growth. Really, how much of what you have been spending is to replace members you have lost? The answer to this question should give you all you need to know about the futility of that path.

If you want the different membership-life experience that comes from becoming a Member Leader, you need to embrace doing just about everything differently. Differently than your peers and friends in the business. Differently than how you've always done things before. Differently than your prospective members' worst expectations.

This difference is the difference.

I can assist you, if you truly have the courage and drive. If you dare to be different—dare to become great—go to www.iFixMemberRetentionProblems.com to begin your Retention Point transformation.

When you reach out I'll conduct an in-depth analysis of your membership attraction, Member On Ramp and retention systems. I'll review your retention numbers to identify your three to five "quickest wins" to increase your member retention and grow your recurring revenue. You are welcome to implement my recommendations yourself with your current team. Most people, when they realize the tremendous opportunities they have to grow their recurring revenue, ask me to help them implement their findings as quickly as possible.

There are three levels to the Member Leader Transformation Program. The first option is coaching. I come alongside your team to create an implementation plan for your fastest wins, providing guidance and input every step of the way to ensure the most effective and fastest implementation. Second, many clients ask that I become part of their team as a project manager. I work with your internal team together with my team (with your approval) to keep everyone accountable for implementing your quick wins; this is perfect for organizations that are already busy with priorities and that need extra hands to implement this important revenue growth initiative. And finally, many clients prefer I, together with my cracker-jack team of copywriters and designers, take over the project and implement everything for them, including copywriting and design of their Member On Ramp; this is the fastest way to experience recurring revenue growth.

To qualify, you must have membership income of greater than $10 million annually or have intention and resources to scale beyond $10 million of income within the next year. And, you must be committed to the personal and professional growth of both yourself and key members of your leadership team.

If you qualify, apply for the program by calling 850-222-6000 or visit www.iFixMemberRetentionProblems.com.

Membership Growth Is About the Members You Keep, Not the New Members Who Join

Time to put away my laptop, stow my tray table and raise my seatback to the upright position. I'm glad to be almost home, been a long trip. How did I do? Was my 27 hours of writing a useful investment for you? You can let me know what you think or ask me a question via email to RS@RobertSkrob.com.

Get the latest member retention case studies, fresh examples and the newest tactics implementing my proven strategies for growing your recurring revenue by joining my Membership and Subscription Growth email newsletter list. Subscribe by visiting www.iFixRetentionProblems.com.

Made in the USA
Middletown, DE
03 June 2019